JOHN YAU • POEMS
Genghis Chan on Drums

OMNIDAWN PUBLISHING
RICHMOND, CALIFORNIA
2021

Cover art: Charles Yuen, "Well of Tears," 78 x 60 inches,
oil on canvas, 2003, collection of Clifford Diver,
Lewes, Delaware. By permission of the artist.

Cover & interior design: Shanna Compton

Library of Congress Catalog-in-Publication Data

Names: Yau, John, 1950- author.
Title: Genghis Chan on drums : poems / John Yau.
Description: Oakland, California : Omnidawn Publishing, 2021. | Summary:
"At once comic and cantankerous, tender and discomfiting, piercing and
irreverent, Genghis Chan on Drums is a shape-shifting book of percussive
poems dealing with aging, identity, PC culture, and stereotypes about
being Chinese via a wide range of surprising forms (pantoums and
sonnets) and unlikely subjects, including the 1930s Hollywood actress
Carole Lombard, the Latin poet Catullus, the fantastical Renaissance
painter Piero di Cosimo's imaginary sister, and a nameless gumshoe.
Seemingly without effort, Yau can go from using the rhyme scheme of an
Edmund Spenser sonnet written in the 16th century, to riffing on a
well-known poem-rant by the English poet Sean Bonney (1969 - 2019), to
limiting himself to the words of condolence sent by a former president
to the survivors of a school massacre. Yau's poems are conduits through
which many different, conflicting, and even unsavory voices strive to be
heard"-- Provided by publisher.
Identifiers: LCCN 2021032493 | ISBN 9781632431004 (paperback)
Subjects: LCGFT: Poetry.
Classification: LCC PS3575.A9 G46 2021 | DDC 811/.54--dc23
LC record available at https://lccn.loc.gov/2021032493

Published by Omnidawn Publishing, Richmond, California
www.omnidawn.com   (510) 237-5472
10 9 8 7 6 5 4 3 2 1
ISBN: 978-1-63243-100-4

Also by John Yau

POETRY

Sometimes (1979)

Broken Off by the Music (1981)

Corpse and Mirror (1983)

Radiant Silhouette: New & Selected Work 1974–1988 (1989)

Edificio Sayonara (1992)

Forbidden Entries (1996)

Borrowed Love Poems (2002)

Ing Grish (2005), with Thomas Nozkowski

Paradiso Diaspora (2006)

Further Adventures in Monochrome (2012)

Bijoux in the Dark (2018)

POETRY (CHAPBOOKS)

Crossing Canal Street (1975)

The Reading of an Ever-Changing Tale (1977)

I Was a Poet in the House of Frankenstein (2000)

Exhibits (2010)

Egyptian Sonnets (2012)

Annals of a Gumshoe (2019), with Trevor Winkfield

Bloken Exhaust (2020), with Branden Koch

FICTION

The Sleepless Night of Eugene Delacroix (1980)

Hawaiian Cowboys (1995)

My Symptoms (1996)

My Heart Is That Eternal Rose Tattoo (2001)

CRITICISM

The Passionate Spectator: Essays on Art and Poetry (2006)

The Wild Children of William Blake (2017)
Foreign Sounds or Sounds Foreign (2020)

COLLABORATIONS

100 More Jokes from the Book of the Dead (2001), with Archie Rand
Big City Primer (1991), with photographs by Bill Barrette
Berlin Diptychon (1995), with photographs by Bill Barrette

MONOGRAPHS

In the Realm of Appearances: The Art of Andy Warhol (1993)
A. R. Penck (1993)
Ed Moses: A Retrospective of Paintings and Drawings, 1951–1996 (1996)
The United States of Jasper Johns (1996)
Pat Steir: Dazzling Water, Dazzling Light (2001)
Joan Mitchell: Works on Paper 1956–1992 (2007)
A Thing Among Things: The Art of Jasper Johns (2008)
William Tillyer: Watercolours (2010)
Jay DeFeo: Chiaroscuro (2013)
Mernet Larsen (2013)
Sam Francis (2014)
Richard Artschwager: Into the Desert (2015)
Catherine Murphy (2016)
Al Taylor: Early Paintings (2017)
Thomas Nozkowski (2017)
California Landscapes: Richard Diebenkorn / Wayne Thiebaud (2018)
Philip Taaffe (2018)
Liu Xiaodong (2021)

EDITOR

The Collected Poems of Fairfield Porter (1985), with David Kermani
Fetish (1998)

For Eve and Cerise

Contents

Prologue

15   Darts and Brooms

I.

23   On Being Told that I Don't Look and Act Chinese

24   After I Turn Sixty-Eight

25   O Pin Yin Sonnet (10)

26   O Pin Yin Sonnet (11)

27   O Pin Yin Sonnet (12)

28   O Pin Yin Sonnet (13)

29   O Pin Yin Sonnet (14)

30   O Pin Yin Sonnet (15)

31   O Pin Yin Sonnet (16)

32   O Pin Yin Sonnet (17)

33   O Pin Yin Sonnet (18)

34   O Pin Yin Sonnet (19)

35   O Pin Yin Sonnet (20)

36   O Pin Yin Sonnet (21)

37   O Pin Yin Sonnet (22)

38   O Pin Yin Sonnet (23)

39   O Pin Yin Sonnet (24)

40   O Pin Yin Sonnet (25)

41   O Pin Yin Sonnet (26)

42   O Pin Yin Sonnet (27)

43   O Pin Yin Sonnet (28)

II.

47   The Congressman's Explanation

48   The President's Telegram

49   The President's Second Telegram

50   The President's Third Telegram

51   The President's First Lesson on Air

52   The President's Asian Menu

53   The President on Playback

54   Broken Sonnet (2)

55   Bloken Exhaust

61   Public Announcement

        III.

65   The Philosopher (1)

66   The Philosopher (2)

67   The Philosopher (3)

68   The Philosopher (4)

69   The Philosopher (5)

70   The Philosopher (6)

71   The Philosopher (7)

72   The Philosopher (8)

        IV.

75   A Painter's Thoughts (1)

76   A Painter's Thoughts (2)

77   A Painter's Thoughts (3)

78   A Painter's Thoughts (4)

79   A Painter's Thoughts (5)

        V.

83   Instructions from the Pantoum

84   Philosopher King

86   Electronic Missive

87   Annals of a Gumshoe

89.   Choose Two of the Following

90   The ABCs of "Of"

92   Poem

93   ·A Flock of Poets

94   The The

95   After Edmund Spenser

96   Suite from an English-Arabic Dictionary

98   Seven Ways to Begin a Business Letter

99   A Case of Mistaken Identity

101   Short Movie Reviews

102   Something to Last a Lifetime

103   After I Turn Sixty-Nine

104   After Wordsworth

105   When It Came to Reading My Future

VI.

109   Latest Weather Report

111   Piero di Cosimo's Sister

113   After Forrest Bess

114   Hotel Jane Alice Peters

116   Hotel de Luxe

117   A View of the Tropics Covered in Ash

118   My Multitudes

VII.

123   After I Turn Sixty-Nine (Second Attempt)

124   The American Way

125   Variation on a Line by Duo Duo

126   Rendezvous

127   For Tom (1944–2019)

129   Unbidden

131   In Memory of My Parents

VIII.

135   The Story of My Beginnings

137   Genghis Chan on Drums

140   Ed's and My Opinion

142   Untitled

143 Untitled (Hotel)

144 After I Turn Sixty-Nine (Third Attempt)

145 For the Spirit of Jean Vigo

146 After Crossing the Mountains in Montale

147 After Rilke

149 Why I Am Still a Poet

150 Abecedarian with Stutter, Written on Bathroom Wall
     of the Apocalypse Lounge

152 Call to Prayer

IX.

155 Catullus Sails to China (1)

156 Catullus Sails to China (2)

157 Catullus Sails to China (3)

158 Catullus Sails to China (4)

159 Catullus Sails to China (5)

160 Catullus Sails to China (6)

161 Catullus Sails to China (7)

162 Catullus Sails to China (8)

163 Catullus Sails to China (9)

164 Catullus Sails to China (10)

Epilogue

167 Nursery Song

169 Nursery Song (Second Chorus)

171 Notes & Acknowledgments

Prologue

Darts and Brooms

1.

When I was a child, every story you told began with the same line: One wants to become a squirrel capable of surviving winter. No one could ever guess what you would say next, which is why we huddled around you each evening and waited for the shadows to walk deeper into the crowded room.

2.

All across the countryside beribboned heirloom bundles of arts and letters began to be stored in broom closets, while the brooms were to put to better use.

According to one of the few surviving chronologies of that turbulent era, this is what happened next. As members of a village or a town (for some reason, cities didn't count), we had to find a new way to measure distance, to anticipate what provisions were needed to travel from Point A. to Point B. It had to be written in a language that we could all agree on, and that knot proved elusive.

In some parts of the countryside it was reported that cookies were banned—a bourgeois luxury signaling that the roots of one's thoughts were planted in the leafy pond of idleness. This was how further roadblocks to wholesome advancement were removed. Elsewhere—though this has proven harder to pinpoint—caravans got stuck in time.

One day we got news from a city seen on the horizon: rows of bobbing smiles were erased from the faces of disgraced instructors. The oldest instructors—the ones closest to being completely useless as opposed to partially useful—were dressed up as scarecrows and brought out to the fields so that they could become one with nature. So began the all-consuming reclamation project—the great upheaval—where barn swallows were trained to peck the eyes of interjectors and those gleaming with inconsequential infirmities.

3.

Your part in this remains a mystery since you were not a direct participant, at least as far as anyone remembers, or even a line of marks in a list included in a citation.

According to a one-eyed witness, there was no moonlight in those years and butterflies lingered outside the park.

One particularly gray Sunday, the body of a battered rabbit was mounted on a stick and planted at the park's entrance as a warning. The meaning of the warning was never agreed upon, which caused waves of consternation to undulate through the gathered clusters, heads bobbing in unison.

It is known that there were other situations where it was best to imitate pigeons but these have not yet been entered into the record.

Monkeys were freed from their manacles.

No one disputes any of these versions since they all have a ring of truth to them, however small and dirty.

4.

Can anyone prove reliable in this environment?

Maybe there is no such thing as an eyewitness.

Who sees the lone mosquito in the dark?

I was there but I didn't see anything.

I heard your eyelids fluttering.

I listened to the sweat rolling off a table.

A beast's fur stiffened against the wind.

A snake slithered out of a jug stored beneath the sink.

The faucet never stopped crying, one pathetic tear at a time.

5.

I listen to your body sinking deeper into the mattress that separates us from the dissatisfied earth. We are not lying next to each in the dark because it is forbidden and we always obey the dictums posted on our doors.

I feel you trembling in the humidity of collective apprehension.

I try to believe that this is a dream scrap floating on a pool of spilled wine.

I don't remember where I read these stories, or if I read them, maybe they just came to me, a memory of my grandmother staring at her reflection, as if she were examining a stranger's pocked countenance.

I was peering into a box full of minor adjustments when it all happened.

I was having an erectile dysfunction when a commotion began taking place outside my window.

I was talking to a rooster or a sheep, someone disguised as a confidant.

The last time I scorned your shadow proved to be our undoing.

6.

The symbol for love is a skull. It does not have to be grinning. It is not a hollow container where you store your jewelry or an orb to be polished by the bedroom window. You should not have told it your secrets.

Those who say poverty finds its own humor are liars, deluded as the mayor on his hands and knees pretending to eat grass.

This is what you never talk about even though it is written all over your face.

Your neighbor was put out to pasture.

You looked at four walls and learned to sew and sing.

Sometimes you would get up and dance.

For years, you took comfort in climbing onto the only table your relatives left behind and pretending that you were looking for the horizon.

I.

On Being Told that I Don't Look and Act Chinese

I am deeply grateful for your good opinion

I am honestly indignant

I am, I confess, a little discouraged

I am inclined to agree with you

I am incredulous

I am in a chastened mood

I am far more grieved than I can tell you

I am naturally overjoyed

I am not going to let you pay me idle compliments

I am not in the least surprised

I am not sure I can manage it

I am persuaded by your candor

I am quite discomfited

I am so glad you think that

I am sorry to disillusion you

I can assure you it is most painful to me to hear you say it like that

I can easily understand your astonishment

I can only tell you the bare facts

I detest exaggeration

I don't know quite why you would say that

I hadn't thought of it in that light

I have never heard it put so well

I see it from a different angle

I stand corrected

After I Turn Sixty-Eight

I find distasteful ways to use the words "enduring" and "hopeful"
I begin stockpiling my daily doses of radiation in an abandoned dollhouse
I order crystals from mail order spiritual specialists and bury them in the front yard
I start telling my neighbors that I am interested in marrying an older mermaid
I ask a coworker if it is unsanitary to sneeze into my unwashed armpits
I confess to the druggist that the condoms are for my besotted dog
I tell the taxi driver that I was lucky to have escaped from the morgue
I shrug my shoulders and pretend that I don't know what you are saying
I ask people if they have seen any strange pedestrians wandering around, dazed
I carry a toy phone under my arm and talk into it whenever I go outside
I once told my psychiatrist that I speak gibberish in four different languages
I pretend that I am poet interested in discarded library books and obscure rhymes
I always sign the guest book with three X's because growing old is pornographic

O Pin Yin Sonnet (10)

"Chinese people can't cry; their eyes aren't big enough."

Their eyes aren't big or straight enough
To let them crocodile slippers slide out
In Eastern Noodle where every dentist is Wong
You can always buy samples of boiled dog squalor
Why should we let them try and keep up with us
How dare they look at us with that impervious squint
Make no mistake these are tight-fisted little marauders
Hollywood assessment got the right narrative for this
You need to kill them off in the first or second scene
Further proof that they will get what is coming
Let them enjoy the fruits of overpopulation
Let their countryside fill with falling sheep
Let them crawl over each other—rapacious bugs think
They can warm their spreading butts on America's corpse

O Pin Yin Sonnet (11)

There is no room for them horizontally
Vertically, or in a jar: glass or ceramic
Even these have started to take up too much room
The confiscation of coffins and urns is a top priority
We must stop the practice of filling the ground
Where there should be factories and high-rises
From now on the dead must be cremated and their ashes
Scattered in a vegetable patch, or by the side of the road
Where they once sat, watching trucks rumbling past
Or scattered on lakes and ponds, wherever they leave
No sign of having once taken up space and now dissatisfied
Wish to leave some part of their husk behind, stubborn coots
Who think their time has not come to an ignoble end
We must pulverize and scatter them and the customs they cling to

O Pin Yin Sonnet (12)

Our joyless eye knows we are not lilies or meteors
But like a caged lion shaking in a cloud of fire
Or a rocket empowered by its own leaves
We become our destiny: military sardines
Side-by-side sliding together in the dark
Our duty: to become slippery and strong
To glide only among our own kind
Like-mindedness is the only goodness
To pray to, suckling judgment on others
Not belonging to our established pride
Join ascending tide or higher tornado
Them being blowhards and we being diehards
We win what is ours: this angry and hungry face
Birth color's pale light draining the migrant air

O Pin Yin Sonnet (13)

"Don't blame bat soup for the Wuhan virus."

They don't just gobble down four-legged and two-legged creatures
They slurp slime-depositing life-forms residing on pond bottoms
They bury their eggs in dirt dug up from children's graveyards
They make broth for dumpling soup from bones of rabid dogs
They scrape donkey hides and turn the piles of pickings into youth jelly
They rub bird droppings into dark crevices in pursuit of yellow beauty
They refuse to change their names to soft letters that roll off the tongue
They hide others among them that harbor torrents of bad and ugly feelings
They claim their ancestors were inventors when they were farmers crouching in mud
They concoct histories so fantastical that not even small children believe them
They invented fireworks, noodles, and kung fu, which hardly adds up to a civilization
They openly sneeze and snicker about it and then scatter like mice
They are nothing more than scribbled names on the flyleaf of a tattered book
They might make good sneakers but they are sneakier than snakes

O Pin Yin Sonnet (14)

We wake to red sky bleeding in its white vest
Like a pair of dice tossed in aftermath of outbreak
You have to praise latest round of questions
Ask if okeydokey ethnic food really that good for you,
Or is it just latest rating hoax, like health food or dieting
Poisoning cerebral contents with stiffened bodies
Filling blessed vessels with undue cravings
You must learn how to stave off naked invasions
When every fork and scrape is another pore of entry
Bugged skin crème burrowing down to matter's heart
Next stop or latest sop: cramped silo offers no asylum
Aren't you tired of falling into traps of advertising
When the less fortunate deserve to be less fortunate
Why limn warning iambics of swarming dread

O Pin Yin Sonnet (15)

We're not talking about Asians; we're talking about China
It is smart business to name a restaurant chain after a cuddly bear
Who happens to be a vegetarian, but it is another thing
To go big-game hunting in the African savanna
I would just as soon turn a panda into a huggy coat or hat.
Importing kudu horns or making a zebra into a rug—
This is real and different. For one thing, it's permanent,
Not just a bowl of green weeds and brown meat scraps
Gobbled, wolfed, or slurped up or jammed down with sticks
Standing beside a dead giraffe that you shot on a hot day
Proves something about the depth of your character
I respect a man or woman that displays big-game trophies
We had Teddy Roosevelt, his Big Stick policy and Rough Riders
What does China have: old men with canes and fallen zippers

O Pin Yin Sonnet (16)

"My message is that let's get back to work.
Let's get back to living.
Let's be smart about it."
    —Texas Lt. Gov. Dan Patrick

The trouble with the Chinese is that they like their old people
The older the better, as if each one of those wrinkled excuses
Was a bottle of fine wine, which they know *nada* about
The Chinese got it all wrong: boatloads of their grandparents
Should be more than happy to die from coronavirus
It's a cost-effective way to save their grandchildren from being poor,
That's why there is something deeply wrong with China and the Chinese
They believe getting old and not working and sitting around toothless
Is proof of love, but it is not; old Chinese are just grinning vampires
Sucking the marrow from their young and packing them off to factories
Americans know better: that's why they go to the beach and play golf
Americans invented plastic surgery, tight pants, and rock 'n' roll
What have the Chinese done besides give us cookies crammed with lies?
We really know how to live, while the Chinese don't even know how to die

O Pin Yin Sonnet (17)

Don't go near them if you want to have a future
Their stores are yellow and flooded with afflictions
Whenever one of them is driving in next lane
I pray they stall and leave this part of the air
This is the only way to translate their stains
Their language wires muddle everything they say
Too many to begin with if you ask the sky
I know some can see out the sides of their faces
Got those shiny black beads and a special tongue
For spotting a wedding ring at the bottom of a lake
Known to sell their daughter's hair to wigmakers
A storm of smooth faces buying up our warehouses
I just don't trust them even when they are honest
Can't you see that there are too many damned races

O Pin Yin Sonnet (18)

(Definitions for Joseph Donahue and Albert Mobilio)

A Senator is a larval form known to sprawl in leather chairs
A wet market is where you go to buy a bucket of unwashed food
A laboratory is what you need to coil together more diseases
A car is the rickshaw you drive when you cannot leave town
A hair salon is a mirror where you breed more germs
A restaurant is a table that lets you sneeze into the food
A President is an elected official who cannot tell the truth to his children
A Secretary of State is a poncho in charge of manufacturing rumors
A housing complex is where you go to die among friends
A sweatshop is one way to help shoppers save money
A whistleblower goes to jail for crimes others commit
A scientist is a shaved baboon who fits neatly into a lab coat
A buffoon is a person who believes the President first
A patriot is often identified by his or her misspelled tattoos

O Pin Yin Sonnet (19)

I would rather be a losing panelist on a game show
Or tied to a folding chair by a one-eared sadist
Open-mouthed, a bird waiting for the drill to descend
I would rather confess my secrets to a psychoanalyst
But if you want to make a bet, I got one you can't lose
They got diseases brewing there that you haven't heard of yet
I wouldn't take home a fortune cookie, no matter how lucky
Don't believe them when they come to you barefoot
Don't believe their alligator tears or their screaming lobsters
They got housing units packed tighter than a pan of burned rice
Living in Chinatown is like living in China
Which is why you should never ever go there
Wuhan is where scaly *Phataginus* vacuums up viruses
Unless you want to exacerbate your syphilis and angina

O Pin Yin Sonnet (20)
(More Definitions)

The Attorney General signs edicts he is not obliged to obey
A Supreme Court Justice speaks the words God puts in his mouth
A Chinese is a robot whose three-syllable name is gobbledygook
A scientist is a person in a lab coat who knows how to spell "doom"
A drug manufacturer knows terrible diseases lead to enormous profits
A man with an AK-47 recognizes that punctuating foreigners is correct
A Senator magically talks out of three sides of his mouth while chewing
A Chinese restaurant is where insidious events are never reported
A news conference is a televised event dedicated to hoods and hoodwinking
A rally is where people proclaim their hatred of those protesting the rally
A country club is where families with servants go to get better service
Golf isn't a game until the loser forfeits either his life or his stock portfolio
A Cadillac cannot be driven smoothly until it has armor plating
Servants who speak good English have become increasingly valuable

O Pin Yin Sonnet (21)

I watched the old man, who is not that old, fall harder than he was pushed
The police walked by because they had seen this act before, many times
They teach it in Chinese circus and acrobat school, an easy trick to get an AHH
I watched the old man, a well-known agitator, a member of a terrorist group
He was carrying something in his hand, a device, probably made in China
Maybe the device sent the wrong signal, causing him to fall backward
That is because Chinese don't read from left to right, but, get this, from right to left
I watched the old man fall, but was the blood coming from his head really his
All you need is a bag you can squeeze and everyone will think you are dying
I watched the old man, who is not that old, act like he had been pushed
After running into the police, tripping over his big feet, and falling backward
One moment he was standing, the next moment he was on the ground bleeding
You don't get that way by being pushed; you get that way by falling
I watched the old man, who is not so old, fall before he was almost pushed

O Pin Yin Sonnet (22)
(Official Instructions)

Condolences are a teaspoon of nonlethal poison injected into sugary cakes

Prayers are a one-size-fits-all set of sweet nothings used in extreme situations

Hearts are recyclable red valentines you send virtually to people who knew the victim

Grief is an incurable disease that afflicts others; always make sure to act sympathetic

Remember to combine words such, as "heartfelt," "sympathy," and "suffering"

Remember to say, "I understand" whenever possible, in the shortest amount of space

Try to act like whatever affliction you are responding to isn't normal and commonplace

You might need to point out that the Chinese don't have words for "pain" and "anguish"

You should not explain that this is why they are inscrutable, and a complete mystery

The Chinese might have other words for grief, but all of them are unpronounceable

When you send a prayer, make sure none of the words are visible to nosy reporters

Condolences are an oversized envelope into which you cram all sorts of knickknacks

Prayers do not need to be memorized since you don't have to say them aloud

Tell everyone the Bible is your favorite book, but don't say which part you like best

O Pin Yin Sonnet (23)

After Shelley

Swarming twits besotted with ill-tempered despot
Sharpening two-edged swords to shield
Themselves from umbrella of sanguine laws
As if time's worst statues could be unsealed
Releasing old, mad, blind, and despised kin
Dragged from smeary dregs of grinning faces
Who string up their enemies in fields of corn
Who believe they are holding an endless run of aces
Who puff leechlike at their bloated country and fling
Till others stoop, bound in blood, without prayer or wing
Wait to be stabbed or shot again in parking lot
Timely as discovering a mobile blood clot
The president suggests we kneel and pray
Hoping to sever our voices from our clay

O Pin Yin Sonnet (24)

Perhaps he should learn not to point and gloat
Why does he keep saying I belong in a boat
I don't think he has ever worn black or told a joke
Do you think he knows what it means to be funny
Did I mention that he often resembles a bunny
He's slipped into obese from burgers and coke
Do you think he keeps small stuff like their G-string
You would think all he ever does is lift his back leg
He sees conspiracies sprouting from every egg
Does he really believe they are all named Sing
That they like to eat food that keeps its features
That they got the extra hots for foul-smelling creatures
His second ex said he has got a heart of chrome
Thank goodness I don't have to stick him in a poem

O Pin Yin Sonnet (25)

(What I see in your eyes)

We are not going to hand anything over
We will continue to blanket the sky
With our mirrors and watch the smoke gallop
See more of your blood falling from the air
Pray fire writes itself into your hands
That whatever words you use will be erased
Make it impossible to wear love on your sleeve
Name on your shirt, heart in your mouth
While you are shouting about nails
Tingling your tongue, what it is like
To hang in the smiles blossoming on
The faces of those who oppose your existence
Your emotions are neither viable nor reliable
Leave yourself behind, but do not speak when spoken to

O Pin Yin Sonnet (26)

We want to be rambunctious and harass anyone who is slow
One way is to play tag with old people and shout at them
They are easy to pick out and they aren't going anywhere
You just need one and the really round ones make good posts
They are fat and slow because they eat fatteners and don't exercise
Imagine one of them trying to run; it might almost make you cry
When standing outside and laughing with friends is more amusing
Only old people and those with weak immune systems die from it
What's wrong with a little horseplay—we're just having some fun
It's always in the back of my mind that the world is freaking out
It's not like they have anything better to do in the summer sun
You can't start sobbing because gray wrinkled people croak from it
It makes a great plot for a revenge film that all the young dream of
It's another good reason to gather outside, drink and sneer

O Pin Yin Sonnet (27)

I talk to a slice of white bread I have been handed
I should learn to be more patient because my time will come I tell it
I ought to be a little thankful for what I have and stop whining
I need to remember this lesson before it is too late
I have never used the phrase "fair enough" unless I am lying
I should know better to act like this and it is a pity that I don't
I must have had parents who did not teach me the meaning of good manners
I can breathe the cool air and that should be more than adequate but it isn't
I don't know what I did wrong but it must have been something really big
I can't blame the weather because it always screwed up my plans
I don't know how I ended up in this position even if I deserve it
I cannot escape my thoughts and every murmur eventually returns to me
I have voices in my head telling me things you might want to hear
I dream about flames, technology, and crumbs floating to the surface

O Pin Yin Sonnet (28)

They cannot say that they invented the atom bomb
They keep crickets in cages and listen to frogs
They don't like to use a knife and fork
They don't drink milk and prefer to eat pigs
They use a different horoscope than the one in the Sunday newspaper
They cry when no one is looking and they don't count their tears
They don't write words that can be translated into English
They brush in their suns with dusty black ink
They know how to stop juices from flowing to the brain
They claim to have invented spaghetti but they don't eat waffles
They like to keep their old people alive as long as possible
They venerate the dead as if they were still sitting beside you
They spit on the sidewalk while talking with their friends
Their hair is great for wigs and they are good at manicuring

II.

The Congressman's Explanation

If you live in your car, I don't have to worry about you not being able to pay rent
If you eat scraps from a dumpster, I don't have to worry about you stealing food
You don't deserve to put in your miserable mouth and fumbling with your rotting teeth
If you find temporary employment in a warehouse so big
That no one remembers your name
I don't have to worry about you thinking your life is shit
Others with name tags will help you reach that conclusion
And if they have any brains sitting fat inside their misshapen skulls
They will inform you that you should have been left out in the rain
Because you didn't save for a rainy day
It's the American way—everyone gets what they merit
You got here on your own, didn't you?
Is it my fault that you failed miserably at being human?
That you became another blossoming eyesore on the scrubbed face of this great nation
There is a good reason that you were drubbed and you know
Deep in your worm-riddled heart that you got what you earned
If you live in your car, I don't have to worry about where you will sleep at night
If you live in your car, I won't have to concern myself
With where you will be found once you are dead
Another petty thought that takes up too much of my precious day
When I have the untrammeled happiness of my constituents to think about
If you live in your car, I don't have to worry about the next election
Because you will be gone, one way or another

The President's Telegram

No child or teacher should ever feel terrible in an American school
My prayers should feel safe to the victims of a terrible child
My condolences to the families of anyone else
Should anyone feel unsafe in school, my condolences
Should anyone feel unsafe in a family, my prayers
Should anyone else ever feel unsafe, my prayers and condolences
Should my prayers feel unsafe, my condolences to the terrible school
Unsafe child and unsafe teacher feel my prayers

(February 14, 2018)

The President's Second Telegram

Unfortunately, early reports of school not looking good
Unfortunately, this loss of decades has been going on too long
We're with you forever in the sadness school
We're affected by this absolutely terrible heartbreak hour
We send our love to everyone affected by our country
We send the loss of life our horrific deadly forever
We grieve for years of heartbreak in this tragic attack

(May 18, 2018)

The President's Third Telegram

There are no words to express
the horrible hour that happened

Journalists, like all fear, should be
attacked while doing their jobs

To the families of the violently,
there are victims who regret your loss

My job is to pledge eternal support
for our horrible sorrow

When you are suffering
we always remember

to pledge warmest
Best Wishes

(June 29, 2018)

The President's First Lesson on Air

It's true. I know bird graveyards better than anybody
I've studied killing bald eagles better than anybody
living in our universe, in Germany, or under a windmill.
If you own a house based on wind, I know you manufacture
a tremendous amount of fumes, spewing noisy carbon
into the atmosphere. I know. I've studied killing better than anybody.
Whether it's in China or your house and the television goes off
I know dead birds are spewing cancer from the graveyards of our tiny world
into our air, our wind, our everything. Congratulations, they say.
Congratulations on your tiny world full of windmills and air

December 23, 2019

The President's Asian Menu

1.

I think the Chinese are a whirlwind they went past
We just got to wait until it catches up with them

2.

The Chinese have not done much in the last hundred years
Before that, they invented fireworks and animal crackers
Climate change is their latest hoax

3.

I like the Chinese, I really do
but I won't eat their food
unless they put ketchup on it
and delicately place it
between the full lips of a hamburger bun

4.

China is just an unfortunate mood
that hasn't passed quickly enough

The President on Playback

My thoughts are no longer with you
They might never have been with you

I will never know, nor should I know
if my thoughts were with you at any time

or if you never thought of me
before you stopped thinking for good

Broken Sonnet (2)

The president is speaking again, his face shining
its blonde lantern from center of cerulean screens
hanging in departure lounges, but no one is listening
They are too busy looking at an azure suit and crimson tie
sections of combed yellow hair lifting into wind's mouth
hands zigzagging, while mouth tries vainly
to dance in time with finger jabbing at soft air
This is our story, he tells each camera
I am a corn-fed miracle, which you cannot say
of my predecessors, who I am not mentioning
even though I have every right to spell out
the parameters of my unbelievable victory,
because from this day hence, even if no one credits me,
you will equate my name with every invisible enemy

Bloken Exhaust

Don't sell me
you don't
already know
forgiveness
is a fantasy
perpetrated
by
bygone
clueless
homeopaths
on path
to yellow
road warrior
beetles
on and on

Wet
red
fire hydrant
light
on spoken corner

Apricot bricks

Cracked sky
in blue mirror
Torn poster of
quivering bellies

More pigs
barking
into their drums

Why call this
splattering
humanity
when it is
freely a crime
to make sure
the godforsaken know
they are forgotten

It's the triumph of the clouds
following the way of the people
spilling multicolored parables
like there is no tomorrow
nearer the truth
than the meticulous pants
I am wearing

                    navy blue
                    sky torpedo
                    in my sleek
                    take-out
                    Mexican enchilada

You stopped here
on hobbled knobbies
another broken start
to this year's seasoning
has been delayed
until further reviews

await me and my
oft-quoted kindness

Unspent
selfish
clench
falling
on your
knees
won't yelp
You just
become
another
houseplant
an alarm clock
waiting for
hysteria
to kick
your bells
a child praying
for the paw
to descend

Don't scurry back into darkness
I have penciled in
all the tears you will ever need
in this lifetime or the next
a whole day's worth of words
nodded and eaten down to their stones

I have promised to place
a potato in your spot
and make up the margins

you swell on
This is what you paid me to steer

People on welfare reserve every nothing they get
Only mules wear perfume to a costume ball
My impatience is a billboard for believing in destiny
I know everything there is to know
about wisdom and its irresistible requirements
I commission the sky to try and match my storehouse
I gain wealth the way the less fortunate add pounds
I don't need permission to chop off your air

The difference between
me and me and me
is I don't call on my muse
when I need an excuse
to regenerate another style
that rhymes
with basic living requirements

I prefer ostentatious and the gold standard
What do you got
I have got all my mouths to take care of, and then some

Nothing you do matters unless it praises me to my proper heights

Who needs monuments
when I am all the living testimony
you are looking for in this air and chalk dust

Bone clap yourself
Plug into the terminal for inexpensive living

Find an affordable proctor for your self-examination
Cry a secure line of credit to the depths of your despicable heart
but fling the arrows of outrageous fortune
and you will find only me
smiling
big face
at the end of your hope

Don't you get tired of braying
in the eternally pulverized
benevolence of your bamboo cart
on a long day's journey to nowhere

There are no strings for you
to pull or tug on
poor puppet-face horde

So many more scores to settle you
if only you would dutifully glisten
in the moonlight of your misgivings

Listening isn't hard once it fades out

Earning your place in the bland scheme of winged idiots is your birthright

I got what I was given and you don't get to taste it
Not even a drop to wet you further than you deserve
I am not just your president; I am your savior

The best you can do is stand
half-baked in the casket
I have so thoughtfully provided

It is my birthday
You can begin
by lighting the candles
starting with your hair

Public Announcement

The next stop is for passenger pick-off or drop down

III.

The Philosopher (1)

He sacrificed the vulgar prizes of life but his eyes danced with velvet spleen
He threw out phrases of ill-tempered humor but trod the path of primrose dalliance
He was often empty of thought but remained entangled in paradox
He gave away his youth by the handful but hurrying thoughts clamored for utterance
He was profoundly skeptical but utterly detached from any sign of obstinacy
He went hot and cold but would fall into the blackest melancholies
He writhed with impotent humiliation but his blank gaze chilled you
He smiled with fatuous superiority but was often stunned and uncomprehending
He made a loathsome object and was afflicted with high levels of metal depletion
He delivered a series of monosyllabic replies but parts of him throbbed recklessly

The Philosopher (2)

He murmured a civil rejoinder shortly before immersing himself in grave thoughts
He never wore an argument to tatters and was known to reenact mysterious ailments
He sat on thorns in the belief that it would set his cumbersome imagination adrift
He sighed deeply from a kind of mental depletion before smiting his snoring neighbor
He stiffened his face into an icy edifice so his thoughts could clamor for more attention
He was aware of the one emotion that caused his limbs to run to marble
He was detached from life even when his face was illuminated by extraterrestrial thought
He gave her a baffled stare while pausing to embrace a sudden daydream
He felt an unaccountable loathing lurking in the rebound of her words
He had a colorless fluency that flummoxed others who were stumbling and silent

The Philosopher (3)

He believed his eyes shone with the pure fire of a great purpose
He always waited until his scorn expired before attempting to speak
He introduced the coaxing inflections of a child into his weekly lecture
He was mistrustful of what any sign of zeal might to do to his argument
He pretended he needed to shamble away in order to encourage further sympathy
He advertised his passions with sneers and pretended to hide behind an exultant smile
He enjoyed what enticements came his way with astonishing unscrupulousness
He airily lampooned his colleagues' most cherished accomplishments
He needed to makes sure he did not release unguarded adjectives into the air
He was the author of books no longer pertinent to the discussion

The Philosopher (4)

He had become a red scalloped cloud hanging motionless in the sky
He grew contemptuously indifferent to the logic of public opinion
He knew his best thoughts were covered with rare vegetation
He was stuck between formless verbosity and passionless rhetoric
He refused to be jaded by his extravagant gastronomical exertions
He felt an unaccountable loathing at his need to toss off ill-humored phrases
He did not want to fall prey to listless uneasiness or eager hopefulness
He was afraid he was a filament in a sea captain's hostile imagination
He expressed surprise by becoming a comical and deferential satyr
He would never again be a poet walking in a valley populated by shadows

The Philosopher (5)

He is an apostle of scorn whose dilapidations have started shaping his recent outbursts

He has not always been deficient in the impulses that we call affectionate or tender

He claims he can convince his audience by flashing an extremely contemptuous veneer

He rejects all charges of incompetence by affirming that he was once afflicted by shyness

He likes to exaggerate his gallantry by adopting a tone of unexpected surprise

He might be a poor dissembler and ludicrously wrong but his humor is not abominable

He is overjoyed—to the point of tears—when he hears himself being quoted by a stranger

He likes to disarm his enemies by comparing himself to a fire hydrant

He feels it is to his advantage to remain imprisoned in a circle of mortification

He confesses to wandering in a mist of vegetal memories whenever the mood suits him

The Philosopher (6)

He is often depicted as a frail exhalation walking under a capricious shadow
He was the first to claim that ecstasy was sustainable under the right circumstances
He possesses a dexterity of phrasing that doesn't require much turnaround space
He has become a creature of circumstantial despair and distorted symmetry
He is known to carry a holiday or two in his eye and gossip in every step
He decided it was to his advantage to become a shuddering green hill
He occasionally feels legions of momentary jealousies prickling his sluggish blood
He has long been possessed by a shameless contempt for gravity
He carries additional supplements of excessive flattery and adulation at all times
He is able to lapse into fits of abject pathos whenever he senses the slightest threat

The Philosopher (7)

He liked to claim that being deceitful was a useful ploy under the right circumstances
He possesses traits that others in his field are loath to discuss in public
He foolishly marries supplemental doubts to the baggage he carries with him at all times
He said he was a form of rust spreading its invidious presence into every discussion
He wrote a theory that proved insoluble, causing his rivals to burst out and celebrate
He was said to be wantonly and detestably unkind, which added to his poisonous allure
He recognized with a vanquished and weary sigh that insights were alien to his spirit
He refused to admit that he had left the rosy twilight of his boyhood in an oily ditch
He knows that his words will outlast him, helping to further diminish his reputation
He compared himself, not unfavorably, to a frying pan crammed with hissing matter

The Philosopher (8)

He partook of the breathless hours phantom governments stole away
He drowsed on his reserved bench between seminars—a fat happy moth
He began making far-reaching sounds, like a shipload of cats in a storm
He had become, in his words, the lingering shudder of a doomed soul
He was, he told a student, a newly waxed floor gleaming in moonlight
He never mentioned that the screeds of others had trampled over him
He often compared himself to a feeble skier waiting for an avalanche
He told us that the breastplate of righteousness had no place in the classroom
He said the dark hours are never swept away, even when they are ashes
He reminded us that sometimes that you must look at the world with a dead face

IV.

A Painter's Thoughts (1)

After William Bailey (1930–2020)

I want to paint in a way that the "I" disappears into the sky and trees
The idea of a slowed down, slowly unfolding image held my attention

Variations on a theme are of no interest. A bowl and cup are not ideas.
I want my painting to be what it contains: it should speak, not me

The idea of a slowed down, slowly unfolding image held my attention
I paint things made of clay, just as the pigments I use come from the earth

I want my painting to be what it contains: it should speak, not me
Brown and ochre stoneware bowls beside a white porcelain pitcher

I paint things made of clay, just as the pigments I use come from the earth
I place the pale eggs on a dark, unadorned tabletop and let them roll into place

Brown and ochre stoneware bowls beside a white porcelain pitcher
The dusky red wall is not meant to symbolize anything but itself

I place the pale eggs on a dark, unadorned tabletop and let them roll into place
I want to paint in a way that the "I" disappears into the sky and trees

The dusky red wall is not meant to symbolize anything but itself
Variations on a theme are of no interest. A bowl and cup are not ideas.

A Painter's Thoughts (2)

After Neo Rauch

I do not plan anything. I just start. Unintentional as a plant
It is as if I am sitting in front of a white wall of fog

The head flitting on a sink: it used to be a broken stamp
I begin with three colors—strange, suggestive and timeless

It is as if I am sitting in front of a white wall of fog
At some point, I must decide to walk into it

I begin with three colors—strange, suggestive and timeless
What I regard as a private matter must be dragged across the canvas

At some point, I must decide to walk into it
What I do has to be unsuitable for anything programmatic

What I regard as a private matter must be dragged across the canvas
The most favorable situation is when a phantom bird disappears

What I do has to be unsuitable for anything programmatic
Time should not be measured with a ruler but a scale

The most favorable situation is when a phantom bird disappears
I do not plan anything. I just start. Unintentional as a plant

Time should not be measured with a ruler but a scale
The head flitting on a sink: it used to be a broken stamp

A Painter's Thoughts (3)

After Suzan Frecon

All decisions are made for visual reasons. The cathedral is finally anonymous
Made of multiple dimensions that go on and on. Even the sky temporarily recedes

I wish to strengthen the painting, make it exist, so that we will want to keep looking
When I traveled, I observed the vast range of red earths in the land and architecture

Made of multiple dimensions that go on and on, even the sky temporarily recedes
Red earth has been used throughout time: there are dots and handprints in caves

When I traveled, I observed the vast range of red earths in the land and architecture
My daughter, the poet, was reading excerpts from a Chinese poem over the phone

Red earth has been used throughout time: there are dots and handprints in caves
I think they are most successful when you can't say they look like something

My daughter, the poet, was reading excerpts from a Chinese poem over the phone
I would love it if I could capture something comparable in my paintings

I think they are most successful when you can't say they look like something
I grew up on an orchard, I was eating plums, and the colors stayed in my mind

I would love it if I could capture something comparable in my paintings
All decisions are made for visual reasons. The cathedral is finally anonymous

I grew up on an orchard, I was eating plums, and the colors stayed in my mind
I wish to strengthen the painting, make it exist, so that we will want to keep looking

A Painter's Thoughts (4)

After Catherine Murphy

My work is about looking very intently—the little curve that follows me
The difference now is that I might dream of an image that I want to do

I woke up as I was putting the blanket on the ground. I understood why I loved it
I am an observer, not a storyteller. I make narratives based on metaphor

When I see something that I want to do, nothing stops me from doing it
Some people want to make the equation narrower, but I want to make it larger

I am an observer, not a storyteller. I make narratives based on metaphor
I want the viewer to understand that this is a painting, not life

Some people want to make the equation narrower, but I want to make it larger
It was written down in a ledger that I was going to be put here to make those paintings

I want the viewer to understand that this is a painting, not life
The form repeats itself, but if I repeat a subject, I would have betrayed it

It was written down in a ledger that I was going to be put here to make those paintings
I could make very pretty brushstrokes, but they have no electrical meaning for me

The form repeats itself, but if I repeat a subject, I would have betrayed it
My work is about looking very intently—the little curve that follows me

I could make very pretty brushstrokes, but they have no electrical meaning for me
I woke up as I was putting the blanket on the ground. I understood why I loved it

A Painter's Thoughts (5)
After Thomas Nozkowski (1944–2019)

I want my ideas to be located at the tip of my brush. Everything must talk back to me.
The idea of a night sky in the Adirondacks and a birch tree—a simple piece of nature

I get a feeling from what I am doing that I am looking sideways at something
Nothing is ever played out; things just lay dormant waiting for another chance

The idea of a night sky in the Adirondacks and a birch tree—a simple piece of nature
Every artist has little rules or devices that enables them to move forward

Nothing is ever played out; things just lay dormant waiting for another chance
If a city has to be geometric, let it become that in the procedure of thinking about it

Every artist has little rules or devices that enables them to move a painting forward
Even if its paintings with faces kissed away, devils scratched off by fingernails.

If a city has to be geometric, let it become that in the procedure of thinking about it
We recognize a friend when he's a tiny mark on the horizon. I like having it both ways.

Even if its paintings with faces kissed away, devils scratched off by fingernails.
I want my ideas to be located at the tip of my brush. Everything must talk back to me.

We recognize a friend when he's a tiny mark on the horizon. I like having it both ways.
I get a feeling from what I am doing that I am looking sideways at something

V.

Instructions from the Pantoum

When I woke up, I did not listen to what the poem told me to write down
I was being led into a defused pachinko shrine guarded by dire wolves

The poem claimed its author was Yellow Money and that everyone was acting foolishly
Rain-cloaked streets, dirty underwear posters, and stenciled exhaust pipes

I was being led into a defused pachinko shrine guarded by dire wolves
The poem added a soft-core soundtrack of copulating lizards falling to earth

Rain-cloaked streets, dirty underwear posters, and stenciled exhaust pipes
I joined the rubbish collection and became a bag of rusty bread

The poem added a soft-core soundtrack of copulating lizards falling to earth
The advance notices were awful but we continued trekking through the gray snow

I joined the rubbish collection and became a bag of rusty bread
The villagers decided the poet needed to play a bugle in her bungalow

The advances notice were awful but we continued trekking through the gray snow
The fish let it be known that they were not happy in their new city-sponsored aquarium

The villagers decided the poet needed to play a bugle in her bungalow
When I woke up, I did not listen to what the poem told me to write down

The fish let it be known that they were not happy in their new city-sponsored aquarium
The poem claimed its author was Yellow Money and that everyone was acting foolishly

Philosopher King

Being a backyard philosopher means you never have to leave the premises

You can patrol the perimeter extolling virtues of mastodons, mugwumps, and manatees

You can claim you are engaged in a lifelong search for the perfect self-reproach

You can use words such as "deleterious," "detrimental," and "counter-reductive"

While underscoring that you know the real difference between a pencil and a penis

That you are familiar with human considerations that lever the world

That you are nearly dizzy with insights and dispensable bits of collectible wisdom

That you can appear to be as irrepressible as a vending machine on a college campus

With cheeks as soft as July peaches touched by winter's chilly breath

Being a luminary means you are invited to festivals and televised appearances

You get to stand beneath a huge sign on which your name appears

You get to pose with your admirers as long as they remain good-tempered

Bow with proper awe and merrily recede into the darkness at the proper moment

Being a backyard philosopher means that you are invited

To throw a beam of light on an unfortunate situation

To explain why termination of different kinds are an outcome of natural forces

That the difference between a pencil and a penis is more than just a few letters

Being a distinguished member means you get to sit at a table with a white tablecloth

That you get to tell costumed individuals what they should bring you

That you can promise to help transform their suffering into a shining beacon for others

Being a spokesperson is a serious endeavor that should never be taken lightly

You are the face of something monumental and therefore frozen in time

You are an artifact retrieved at a later date and used as a reference point, a marker

You are invited to festivals as a human machine undergoing upgrades

Being invited to festivals means you get to sit at a table with starched white tablecloths

That bugs and other forms of living nuisance are gently shooed away, at your request

But are never deliberately harmed because that would mar your beatific visage

Being seated at a table with a white tablecloth means you are a serious endeavor

Being a serious endeavor means you are a distinguished member and important

That you know the difference between a pencil and a penis is more than slippery sound

Electronic Missive

All my friends have at one time or another told a long pointless story about their aunt Millie, Maddie, or Moo. She likes to drink martinis with an olive and two onions, stand at the kitchen window and talk to the birds she wanted to poison last summer, bellow at Uncle Buck, go to the dog track in a taxi (she hates horses and might be allergic to them), spend Sunday mornings painting her toenails either viridian or midnight blue, collect ceramics of frogs playing the violin, which, I recently heard, is more popular in certain geographical swaths of America than reading a book of confessional poetry borrowed from the local library. There is no statistical proof of this, of course, but Aunt Matilda is convinced that if her nephew becomes a poet, he is fated to die of blood poisoning caused by ingrown toenails, the result of sitting alone in a darkened room, pondering which word to use next. The fact that I do not have any aunts or uncles has never prevented people I thought knew me better than they obviously do from going on about a colorful relative of theirs whose story they think I will find interesting, amusing, or disgusting. This is why I am sending this mass email. I no longer want to hear any stories about distant relatives— especially aunts and uncles. I think the world is awful enough without having to hear about people who go on living their miserably cheerful lives in far-off locales with names like Omaha, Madras, Mudcluck or Massapequa. I do not need to know what goes on outside this room. I am perfectly content to be where I am. And yes, my toenails are perfectly fine, thank you very much.

Annals of a Gumshoe

This is in honor of gumshoes and the ragged black circles (or flattened eye patches) we see on sidewalks, remnants of a bygone era.

Gumshoes walk the streets even though gum is no longer found sticking to gray sidewalks.

Gum is gone, like the telephone booth, the cheap suit, and a president you could believe in part of the time, but the gumshoe lives on, nearly extinct, a black or albino rhinoceros wandering nervously up and down the honking streets of a busy metropolis, sidewalks jammed with people talking on cell phones, not looking at where they are going, or smiling at the camera they hold in front of them, a silver slice of apple at the end of an adjustable pole.

The gumshoe does not realize that even though he is a rhinoceros, he is invisible—like a Chinese person in China. No one will ever want to stand beside him and be photographed.

The gumshoe hates Gertrude Stein, who is rumored to have written, "a gumshoe is a gumshoe is a sum of goo," but as no one has ever claimed to have read every word that she wrote, there is no absolute proof that these words are Stein's and not someone else's, possibly someone known as Delphinium Blue or Giorgio Scarlett, a writer whose modest reputation has dwindled down to a name cited at a party full of drunken poets, some of whom are heartbroken.

The gumshoe stands in doorways. He believes in taxis, preferably in a primary color or white or black. He carries a set of precision tools he knows will help him get into any prewar apartment, but is constantly thwarted by hotels and the electronic activated cards they issue to guests and reward-winners. He wonders why he no longer gets hired to go through drawers of women's underwear in search of a telltale clue, forgetting there are now exclusive clubs for this and sundry other misdemeanors. Due to a small twitch in his left cornea, he constantly confuses the phrase "dairy farmer" seen on the sides of trucks with the words "diary armor," which he has been looking for without much success.

The gumshoe likes to wake up in the middle of the night and look out the window, but often wonders whatever happened to air shafts and movie theaters with painted ceilings and velvet curtains.

Whenever he is out, walking the streets, the gumshoe pretends that he is a poet, an occupation he believes is poised closest to the chute of obsolescence down which we will all eventually plunge. He goes out searching for poems, the unexpected moment of illumination, the instance of perfect madness. He sits on park benches and listens to the long-suffering, the cheerful, the explosive and the bragging. He begins making a mental list of all the uses a dentist's hairbrush might be put to. He is happy to be one of the few who can sit in a park and not be tormented by flies and bees. He realizes that heightened moments of cognitive recognition no longer come in handy. He is glad he does not have to stand behind a podium and talk about the origin of the Opium Wars or the Poetry Wars, which he knows even less about. He smiles brightly as he fondles his stolen cookie.

Choose Two of the Following

We acknowledge with audible pleasure the receipt of your most recent complaint
We readily admit that you are justified in your attempt to solicit another opportunity

We are anxious to make you understand why we are not at your service at all times
We are confident that you will have no further trouble making sizable concessions

We readily admit that you are justified in your attempt to solicit another opportunity
We assume our exceptional confidence expresses the proper level of appreciation

We are confident that you will have no further trouble making sizable concessions
We realize that this is simply an unavoidable oversight on your part

We assume that our exceptional confidence expresses the proper level of appreciation
We regret that we are unable to correct the matter of your disappointment

We realize that this is simply an unavoidable oversight on your part
We have discovered that this misstep required us to adopt harsher measures

We regret that we are unable to correct the matter of your disappointment
We quaff mugs of delight while recounting the details of your latest inconvenience

We have discovered that this misstep required us to adopt harsher measures
We will be glad to render you any assistance that isn't too costly

We quaff mugs of delight while recounting the details of your latest inconvenience
We acknowledge with audible pleasure the receipt of your most recent complaint

We will be glad to render you any assistance that isn't too costly
We are anxious to make you understand why we are not at your service at all times

The ABCs of "Of"

1.

Aberrations of meanness
Absence of ignominy
Acquisition of attention
Age of brain
Agility of despair
Anachronisms of moderation
Annulment of manners
Ardor of opinion
Austerities of brutality
Avalanche of ignorance

2.

Babel of exclusion
Ban of enthusiasm
Barriers of fact
Beam of prey
Bewilderment of portraiture
Bliss of fate
Bone of civility
Bouts of law
Brow of disgrace
Burden of confidence

3.

Cadences of confusion
Calmness of passion
Careless of solicitude
Chaos of evidence
Chorus of hills
Code of calamities
Community of imagination
Courage of hospitality
Crash of contempt
Curl of delirium

Poem

Poem drifting past rows of unopened eyes
Poem arising from depths of unimaginable bitterness
Poem constructed from unimpeachable sentiment
Poem riddled by unmelodious echoes
Poem unsettled by uproarious fripperies

Like the faint cry of music disheveled by the wind
Like jewels gleaming at the bottom of a lake on a moonless night
Like a vase in which roses offer further proof of immortality
Like lighting a candle in a lifeboat at twilight
Like flecks of foam gathering on the strings of an unknown musical instrument

A Flock of Poets

Dora Doll slips through a hole in the poem's tent and becomes a hedgehog.
Is this any way to begin an epic—a grape Popsicle stuck to a dog's spotted tongue?

Daedalus squats in a bar telling stories of his last flight; he never uses the word "sun."
Another robot angel—or is it angel robot—claims the coveted crown of poet accountant.

Is this any way to begin an epic—a grape Popsicle stuck to a dog's spotted tongue?
Bucket of bad hooch, coldhearted twit, aspirin machinist, and babbling gravel washer.

Another robot angel—or is it angel robot—claims the coveted crown of poet accountant.
Do you want to end up as an unemployed centaur crunching down leftover dog food?

Bucket of bad hooch, coldhearted twit, aspirin machinist, and babbling gravel washer.
What happens when the poem goes stale and you are left holding the punishment bag?

Do you want to end up as an unemployed centaur crunching down leftover dog food?
What does it mean to be a celebrated glue maker if nothing holds together?

What happens when the poem goes stale and you are left holding the punishment bag?
I think you would have had more luck being a soothsayer or a scavenger

What does it mean to be a celebrated glue maker if nothing holds together?
Dora Doll slips through a hole in the poem's tent and becomes a hedgehog

I think you would have had more luck being a soothsayer or a scavenger
Daedalus squats in a bar telling stories of his last flight; he never uses the word "sun."

The The

The inaccessible solitude of loveliness heard at evening
The indefinable yearning for soot and pyramids
The intercepted glances of high-strung selfishness
The irrevocable past running downhill to the sea
The low hills on the horizon of monotonous despair
The meticulous observation of formless dread

After Edmund Spenser

The wind rewrites your name in sand
And with voluptuous flair scrapes it away
Who else offers you an invisible hand
Is it only vanity to want to write an essay
Which will do its job: immortalize
Each step of your imminent decay
Which you is you today—prey or pray
Let the wind swirl your name likewise
Believe what you want: everything you devise
Shall crumble to dust; you will never gain fame
For the wind is all you have to eternize
Your bodily summation in a common name
Folly to think the world is a monster to subdue
That no matter what, it will return and renew

Suite from an English-Arabic Dictionary

1.

Birth at term

Birth attendant

Birth control

Birth defect

Birth grant

Birth intervals

Birth kit

Birth order

Birth postponement

Birth rate

Birth spacing

Birth weight

2.

Soft commission

Soft contract

Soft convertibility

Soft-core pornography

Soft currency

Soft detergents

Soft dollars

Soft energy

Soft goods

Soft landing

Soft law

Soft loan

Soft rime

Soft rock
Soft roe
Soft target
Soft-shell turtle

Seven Ways to Begin a Business Letter

I am not completely impervious to your latest string of packaged compliments
I am not that grateful for your outbursts of indignity
I am inclined to be incredulous over your recent suggestions
I am supremely capable of unraveling your high-toned prejudices at this time
I am neither persuaded by, nor in sympathy with, your alarmist candor
I am not naturally overjoyed by the details of your ambition
I take no satisfaction in imagining something more disagreeable than you

A Case of Mistaken Identity

I told the uniformed kangaroos they had the wrong man and they agreed and let me go. This kind of thing happens to me often—being mistaken for someone else. The kangaroos—who are notoriously nearsighted—were not sure if they had apprehended the right man (a petty criminal), a poor hapless soul (possibly a dishwasher) or, in my case, a white-haired poet known to walk around the city at night, in search of the perfect pairing of cupcakes and congee.

I told them who I was and what I did and they believed me because they never heard such a story before. I wondered what story I would tell the next officers I met. It is best to keep changing your tune when you are in a different circumstance.

By the time I climbed the five flights to my apartment I was another person, a decorated infantryman who had come back to the street he grew up on and was shunned by his family and neighbors because the glories of war no longer had the meanings they once broadcast.

After a few months, I moved away and once again changed my name. I lived in a state ending with "x" and learned to do things with my hands that I did not think was possible. I also learned to fly and went to parties. I stood in the corner and made mental notes, starting with "emesis" and ending with "sniverlard." I began telling everyone how I rated his or her sense of humor on a scale of 1 to 10. Being a strict grader, I made fewer and fewer friends.

In the meantime, I was run over by a car, a freckled boy on a tricycle, and a pilot who wondered why I was lying in the middle of the runway.

I raised dachshunds but did not feed them kitchen scraps, as one future biographer will later claim. Joined to an outmoded battery, I began sparking in the middle of the night until the neighbors decided I should move to another part of town—where this kind of behavior was tolerated and even embraced—and I did. This is why I told the police officers they had the wrong man. They were looking for a man who tried to rob an ATM, not a man who thought he should have been born in a deeper fog.

Short Movie Reviews

It is isn't always gratifying to watch filmmakers indulge their basest impulses
It is sickening to the nth degree as well as audacious and arrogant
It is far from being a well-rounded fiction indebted to the world's hot spots.
It is perfectly trite which isn't always perfectly defensible
It is wonderful how quickly it went past my comprehension
It seems preposterous, a distracting dream, or, at the very least, unspeakably funny
It was an unpardonable liberty that is best forgotten
It is such a bore having to talk about its many virtues
It might sound alluring but it is actually rather unapologetically pathetic
It is deliciously honest, which, I can assure you, is rather troublesome
It will divert your thoughts from any pleasure you might be open to receiving

Something to Last a Lifetime

I used to have many children, almost more than I could count. They trampled through these paneled rooms. They left their toys, dolls and soldiers, lunch pails, books, and clothes strewn about—the way the dead and their gear are scattered across a battlefield photographed by Mathew Brady. There were at least four maybe five of them and they were eight years apart in total, the makings of a surly mob. They got along except when they didn't, which was nearly all the time. They bickered, badgered, and butchered, not necessarily in that order. My wife said that they were copying us, but I disagreed and told her to mind her own business, which she soon did. But now she's gone down into the dirt and the children are spread apart, like bread crumbs praying for the right beak to scissor them away.

I mean I still have children. At least I think I do. I haven't read otherwise or gotten notice. It has been a long time since—perhaps too long but then maybe not long enough, after all.

I remember sitting at the dining room table looking at them—a long row on each side of the table—waiting for me to be funny, make a face, say something smart or tell their mother how much I loved her cooking. I never failed to disappoint them. It was the best advice that I could have ever given them.

After I Turn Sixty-Nine

I don't imagine that a chariot is hurrying near but that a sleek car is speeding up
I have started a list of the costumes I want to be buried in, beginning with horny centaur
I try to put aside obituaries but I am unable to do so for very long (maybe ten minutes)
I eat the same meal night after night while reading recipes of dishes I have never tasted
I shudder nearly every time I read the phrase "Lifetime Guarantee or Your Money Back."
I no longer find it necessary to stop and look at what is going on at a construction site
I decide I won't tell people to stop sending me books even if I will never read them
I stop and watch ambulances trying to get past cars that don't want to move aside
I begin thinking about different methods I might use to remove myself from the story
I know what my friend meant when he said his dog would take his place on the couch
I think about the cities I will never return to, including Cadaqués and Caracas
I wonder when I will no longer begin a poem with the words "if" and "when"
I dream that my ashes will be scattered in a remote spot in Ireland that no one visits
I admit that shrinking into myself is not as unpleasant as I once thought

After Wordsworth

I wandered lonely as a shroud.

When It Came to Reading My Future

You gazed at my palms and said they were lying about what lay ahead.

VI.

Latest Weather Report

We join the bughouse battalion of the Last Salvation Army, climb aboard the purring trucks and head for the valley where the fires still rage. Death rides beside us in an air-conditioned limousine, a big green grin sewn crudely to his otherwise flawless face.

The next morning we stop in a mall to obtain extra rounds of supplies. We are headed for the hollow space on the map from which we are said to have emerged, complete and in ruins. The parking lot is full of empty ambulances and crawling with examples of suburban loneliness. We back away from anyone who shows something resembling a face, knowing it is the residue of plastic surgery.

In the rubble lots we passed, children are busy pulling handfuls of stuffing from armchairs and depositing them in color-coded plastic buckets. Their motto: No waste shall go to waste. This is the economy we have adjusted to, living on what the rich have used and found disagreeable.

We buy only the designated essentials: wizened apples marked by starlike bruises and other signs of holiness; domestic animals that have been injected with preservatives at the moment of their genital illumination; fishbowls full of earthworms; blank dresses and shirts, windowsills to climb over.

Those who fail the daily quiz are relieved of their maps.

Other than hand signals, most communication takes place at night when we can send ants across each other's skin, their six legs tapping out messages. We were taking turns recounting the plots of android vs. zombie movies shortly before dawn stopped and didn't cross the horizon. We got up and began driving.

The mall is a memory fading in a mirror, a relic whose function is no longer apparent.

Death's grin continues spreading across his face.

New reports are being received all the time.

The sun can't be found, but we remain convinced that it hasn't gone far.

Piero di Cosimo's Sister

Pack up your diplomas; they will not help you here. As you have by now gleaned, the information you have gathered from a succession of rapid screens is infected. Archives have been pilfered or riddled with invention; no one is sure which. Inventories are no longer secure.

An armada of green beetles looks down from the ceiling, their knobby stalks devoid of curiosity. As a young apprentice, I had to learn to wash their gloves once they were finished feeding, and hang them in the courtyard to dry. It is not a pleasant chore, but, as time passed, I found myself looking forward to residing in this reassuring cycle of reasonable horror.

Further back, when I was a child, my mother read me the same story time and again, even after I tired of it and began my usual bawling. The admonitions slung to the fetid air. You can trade in your watch with its ninety-nine-year warranty whenever you want. You can adjudicate your gambit and calculate the odds. Or you can elect a program of arid progress, with each forward step illustrated by an assembly of accosted thoughts, but this comes with no suppositories, supplements or backup plans.

Look around. Panoply of shivering nudes surrounds a giant strawberry, its rotting sweetness spilling onto the ground. Owls and ostriches gather under a crystal chandelier. The shorter owls are waiting for another egg to fall, while the taller ostriches plan to bury theirs in the sandbox they have hidden behind a police station.

X marks the spot where the conductor stands, arms flailing about, like an angry mouse.

This is when lethargy finally triumphs, confining me to a padded chair. Once settled, I immerse myself in gadgetry's mattress, happily succumb to pixelated blue's insidious tug. In the foreground, daisies and daffodils, those happy pedestrians, climb the observatory steps. A chorus emerges from the Formica forest, singing: Everyone wants to ascend the ladder with nine rungs lowered from the glowing orbs.

Or this is when you first see the painter enter her studio.

After stopping to scratch the ears of a sleepy satyr, she picks up her brush. With a few quick strokes, she removes the clothes of those waiting to be tossed into a cauldron, their smiles gleaming—like so many fish—beneath a melting sun.

After Forrest Bess

I live at the top of a tower the last regime never got around to demolishing. Each morning, shortly after the sun speaks above the horizon, I ride the temperamental box down from my corner abode, where I live with my grumpy and devoted companions, and walk to what remains of the nearest beachside town. Later, after completing the few tasks I still have left to do—and they have been diminishing with each passing month—I make my way back to the tower and begin climbing the concrete stairs to my room, preferring this mode of transportation to the box's hesitant rise.

This is always my favorite part of the day, the transition from one domain to another. For a long time, I am the only entity moving inside a squared-off column, a concrete silo that houses neither missiles nor grain. It is during this period, when I am cut off from all contact, I actually feel like a meaningful unit capable of contributing to the happiness of articles.

I rise slowly, like a swimmer rising toward the sunlight. There is nothing to see but concrete walls and the numbered doors on each landing. This monotony is what it will be like when I am placed in my reusable coffin and carried to the edge of the extinct volcano that still attracts a few people during the last warm days of summer, before ice begins ascending with silent fury.

After I expend a considerable amount of energy and thought, especially for one whose batteries are from another era, I open the door to my room and announce my return. This is when things get tricky or should I say sticky. This is when I fall back into wondering what secrets my birds happily hide under their black and violet wings.

Hotel Jane Alice Peters

I like sitting in hotel lobbies that are as big as the apse of a cathedral and strung with Christmas lights. I like it when my posterior sinks into the cushion provided by the hotel management for exactly this encounter between lower extremity and nuanced comfort. I like letting my spine and all the flesh that surrounds it fall back into the carefully rounded, slightly tilting support that is attached to an elevated pairing of horizontal cushions that rests securely on four elegantly turned legs. I like the silver claws that form the chair's feet. I like knowing the architecture of this assembly was constructed with human ease in mind. I like pretending that I belong in a lobby festooned with polished brass fixings reminiscent of another era, or framed by fluted marble columns harkening back to an even earlier era. I like knowing I can travel back in time.

This is when I start replaying my favorite interlude, when I begin dreaming of meeting Carole Lombard, who died in a plane crash in Mount Potosi, Nevada, aged 33. This happened on January 16, 1942. Today is January 17, 2019, more than seventy-five years later. Is there a hotel in Mount Potosi? Is it named after Lombard, third wife of Clark Gable?

I like burrowing inside the extinct topography resurrected by young hotel designers, their manufactured version of our collective longing. I like their efforts to harness the barely controllable desire we have to step away from the time we inhabit into a hologram sector that has not been overrun by apocalyptic data. I like knowing that the scar a car accident left on Lombard's face could not be completely erased, and that we can see its trace on her cheek—like a horizon line—when the camera moves in close, as in *Hands Across the Table* (1935), costarring the charmless Fred MacMurray. I like knowing that she did not want to simper prettily or scream in terror on the screen. I like knowing that the "e" was added onto her name by mistake and that she decided to keep it. I like knowing that she took life as it came, even if I am not of that ilk and do not want to go down that tortuous path.

Hotel de Luxe

At night, I deposited myself inside an old refrigerator factory because the town's only hotel had burned down the previous spring. There was a box of outdated candies on a dusty shelf, along with other expired ingredients. It always rained just after daybreak so that the townspeople could readjust the clocks of their melancholia. For several unexceptional passages of time, I slept in an extended bathtub where a baby was said to have drowned. I think this child must have found it necessary to bite its tail and vanish, which is why the tub was empty when the young father returned, having left earlier in the day to watch a horse race. Luck did not smile on him that day nor on any of the others he would endure until his improbable story ended. This, I have been told on repeated occasions, is how the town got its reputation for being chilly to visitors who come here with something to sell, combs or pocket watches made on another island.

A View of the Tropics Covered in Ash

I began lying to myself at regular intervals, stopping by the side of the road only when it was necessary. The vegetation did not improve even as the interludes of pleasant shrubbery and herbaceous plants changed, and the waterfalls eventually became walls smothered in stains. I got tired of following myself back to the place where I was delivered; a howling newborn already indoctrinated that the mandibles of doom awaited me, along with other taunts and temptations too monstrous to mention. I did not have to sit long. We must all make dung, announced the boy with a smile full of crooked teeth. This was in the lobby where the first assignments were handed out. Where did you get those pearly gravestones screamed his toothless sister? What do you mean what do you mean moaned another vehicle headed for bedlam in an elastic waistband.

Life in an upscale suburb isn't bad once you get used to hell. The suburban pageantry of soccer played with plastic skulls and capacious bugs on a green summer day is worthy of an opera, complete with pouting male and curvaceous diva. Drugstores that deliver licensed drugs and pastel condiments are not to be sneezed at. There are plenty of tonics guaranteed to cure baldness, but impotency is something to be proud of, since it means your contributions to civilization's convulsions are dwindling at an accelerated rate.

This is the time to begin concentrating on flying carpets, inexpensive episodes, and sitting in a rowboat on a speckled lake, dreaming of that moment long ago, when the first lie came to you unbidden. You are sleeping under a tree that reaches up past the bottom layer of starlit clouds. The lower branches are burning, just as you planned.

My Multitudes

That blackened winter we came down from the mountains, a ragtag, end-of-the-year collection of shepherds (or wanderers) the city tried hard to herd into holding pens.

My older sister escaped and fled to the forest, which was still burning and safe, while my younger brother (or bother) grabbed a spoon and started digging his way to China.

I grew up in shambles; my pockets crammed with expired ration coupons.

I was a safety hazard, a name spoken only in the dark.

I learned to wear shame and call it the color of my skin.

Saturday afternoon time-wasters formed the basic staples of my ill-conceived diet. Famished youth, I fed myself on a rerun cycle of axe grinders; prison rats; corrupt corrupters; blackmailers; ruffians; embittered siblings; lone wolves and every variety kept on the shelf of angry packs, delivered like candy to be gobbled because it released a burning sweetness as it went down.

At school, I pretended to watch time drop its noose into a simmering ocean until the screen flashed another enticing signal.

Today, as a multiple personality adult in need of more therapy, I try and keep track of babbling chestnuts and overflowing toilets, to clap discreetly at the luminous pageantry of flashing lights, ambulances and police cars, especially.

Don't any blips puddle up your screen? I hear you ask rudely.

Are you wondering where our furry little scapegoat went and how we might go about getting another? I answer.

How is this boatload of strife different from the last delivery, which we are still sorting through? whimper the cowed crowds filling my head.

Today, amidst the crashing voices, my forlorn corpulent self stumbles down darkened lanes, while my other bumpkins and bobbins grow more rowdy beneath the pagoda trees of the infested capital, where the president is content to disguise himself.

The mirror listens to his abbreviated confession. He believes he has been miscast as a petty bickerer rather than as a cheerful baker. Never one to glow in the dark, he relishes splendor only when it comes to him in designer packages. He is a self-made dam, an impregnable wall.

Perhaps this is why you have come to me. Perhaps you are a restless nocturnal spirit looking for an outlet, even as the planes soar overhead, their bomb bay doors flapping.

What multiplication system of bleeding have you refused, knowing better offers are a manufactured dream, a byproduct of our continuous distractions?

Or perhaps you are another troubled twister who wants to make good?

Is that why the words in me are beginning to break ground? Perhaps they are looking for a place to take root, shake off the dust surrounding them.

Cold afternoon. Transient enterprises cancel each other out in this world of shopkeepers and weakened hospitality.

The wind settles into the trees, plump birds waiting to be plucked for their monetary value.

It is nearly tomorrow.

Have you set your alarm, as you know you should?

Have you considered how many other unheard singers are standing beside you in this corner of the incinerator?

VII.

After I Turn Sixty-Nine (Second Attempt)

I am the droop-bellied man who passes himself on the street and doesn't nod

I still possess a shred of wit but will that be enough when the time comes

I know how to spell my name—its seven letters—but that too is beside the point

I carry my expired driver's license because a stranger might need to identify me

I have forgotten my first phone number and do not know who has taken those digits

I still have long talks with you even though I am the only person sitting in the room

I think that I might not be the author of what I am writing or what you are reading

I still see you walking by, never in much of a hurry, and wonder where you are going

I believe that "epic," "cheap muffins," and "full confession" do not add up to a poem

I still wrap my hands around those parts triggered by raw chicken and astrology

I have stopped dreaming about taking a leisurely vacation inside an encyclopedia

I wonder if I will ever stop telling myself that this is the last time that I will ever do this

I continue to think that I was meant to have been a taxidermist driving a taxi in Budapest

I still recall the afternoon—a half century ago—you drove me home and said goodbye

The American Way

Getting old in America
is a laughable achievement
Everyone gets to laugh at you

Dying young is worse

Everyone pretends to cry
secretly happy that you won't
block their rise up society's ladder

Variation on a Line by Duo Duo

I love the house on fire
inviting us to lie down

Inviting us to become
its tightly fitting roof

As if the moon is a python
waiting to uncoil

As if our blushing cheeks
did not offer brazen proof

I love the house on fire
inviting us to lie down

Umber summer falling
slowly to its knees

Inviting us to lie down
in its scarlet tracks

Inviting us to embrace
the already blazing sky

Rendezvous

You hear rumors of impotence, garlands of sobs, and more noise—
A city where tourists stop to talk and draw their outlines in chalk.

When are your contents scheduled to expire? Will you still be here when they do?
I wanted to be a portrait artist until I realized I had to remember a missing face.

I know a city where tourists stop to talk and draw their outlines in chalk.
Gathered beneath soiled clouds—the color of rats when they finally stop running.

I wanted to be a portrait artist until I realized I had to remember a missing face.
You must keep meticulous records of the condensation collected from the tops of leaves.

Gathered beneath soiled clouds—the color of rats when they finally stop running.
What will you do after you boil the last smidgeon sitting in your fridge?

You must keep meticulous records of the condensation collected from the tops of leaves.
I will practice hissing and growling when strangers knock on my door.

What will you do after you boil the last smidgeon sitting in your fridge?
I will glue sheets of bright blue paper to my window. I will close my eyes.

I will practice hissing and growling when strangers knock on my door.
You hear rumors of impotence, garlands of sobs, and more noise—

I will glue sheets of bright blue paper to my window. I will close my eyes.
When are your contents scheduled to expire? Will you still be here when they do?

For Tom (1944–2019)

"No one ever said the world was just."
  —Thomas Nozkowski

I was told I spoke in my sleep but I never heard what I said.
Nor did I wish to listen to recordings of my body whispering in the dark.
The gap grew wider and I could no longer tell which one was me
or if even such a bundle of possibility existed in the pronominal world.
I wondered if the ones who got in the newspapers and were quoted
took themselves as seriously as their carefully described couture.
Sometimes, before opening the door or stepping off the elevator,
I worried how long I would last at the gathering
before I uttered something foul and stupid and slunk off
mad at myself for all the wrong things
including behaving badly once again.
As the years passed, trembling and crying in the dark became easier.
I don't regret my lack of social skills or how I fumble for words.
I came here to write, which means I moved to this city to be alone,
and learned that I was wrong to think that was how it was supposed to be.
I have started to accept my incompetence at the simplest tasks
but I do not disdain worldly glory and sincere praise.
I learned that my many mistakes were radioactive
and I went on planting them while traveling with others
or being pulled along by my brainwashed dog.
I like wine but I don't care for wine-tasting parties
and pretending my smile flourishes in the presence of others.
And yet, whenever I did go out in those youthful
pent-up days of outbursts and foot stomping
I heard people I knew and did not know

talking about a kind and ambitious man
an artist who wasn't bedeviled by an envious personality
who believed in what he did but never bragged about it
who refused to join any clubs that would have welcomed him.
How could such a person possibly exist
in a fallen city of prize-watchers and fading flowers
among teeth gnashers and hair pullers
and those who thought power was the only thing to reach for
as their smiles bloomed whenever someone looked their way?
In time, I learned that the words "gracious" and "generous"
did not reveal how much that man gave to others,
myself included, and who never asked for anything back
nor did he ever talk about what he had done
to make others happy; it wasn't in him
to call attention to himself in that way.
When he was dying, which he was for many years,
he never invited me to notice his condition
never told me how I should feel about what he was enduring
made it ever so gently clear that I should not ask him.
I learned to be more proud and to not remind people
that I had volunteered to serve in the unpaid post of poet.
I thought that if I was here to be a writer
then that is what I should do
regardless of what other people thought about what I did.
I want to tell him these things, even though he is no longer here.
I doubt he would have put up with this description
no matter what the circumstances might be.

Unbidden

I never have been a pallbearer. I did not help carry the coffins of my mother or my father—they died a few months apart—to their adjacent unmarked plots in a fenced-in cemetery on a suburban street near Burlington, Massachusetts, where they and my brother moved after I graduated from high school. Twice, I selected a coffin and paid for it with my credit card, but I never felt the actual physical weight of their death.

It was a bright and sunny morning when my father called. An hour later I was carrying a large cardboard box to the post office. That is when I saw her and did not know what to say when—for the first time—she stopped in front of me, smiled and said: how are you?

We were standing close together, in a zone not quite penetrated by what was around us. We had been smiling at each for weeks, maybe longer—whenever we passed each other, usually on a Saturday on West Broadway when everyone was going to art galleries—but we had never said stopped to say hello to each other before because one of us was always with someone else. I stood there and said: I am well. I am going to the post office and looked at the unwieldy box I was carrying. I gave her a weak smile and a shrug and I walked away and never saw her again.

I left that afternoon on a plane and made my way to my parents' house, a place I stayed in but where I never lived because I did not have a room there. I did not talk to anyone about what had happened. When she said hello and smiled, I was still hearing my father tell me that my mother had just died. He said that the last thing she said to him was how disappointed she was in me, and that I was clearly a failure for a son. A few moments later she had a heart attack and fell down the stairs. He had waited a long time to say these things to me in a calm, matter-of-fact voice, things my mother never said. I could hear him smiling loudly behind his report.

I stood there looking at a woman that I was smitten over and daydreamed about and all I could manage to do was mutter a few meaningless pleasantries.

I walked away.

I walked away wondering: is this what it means to be a poet?

You carry boxes to the post office.

You are tongue-tied and lost.

Whatever you want to say will not be said in this lifetime.

In Memory of My Parents

Streets of Shanghai (1927)
Back from Shanghai (1929)
The Ship from Shanghai (1930)
Shanghai Express (1932)
Charlie Chan in Shanghai (1935)
West of Shanghai (1937)
Exiled to Shanghai (1937)
Shadows over Shanghai (1938)
North of Shanghai (1939)
Halfway to Shanghai (1942)
The Shanghai Cobra (1945)
The Lady from Shanghai (1947)
The Last Ships from Shanghai (1949)

VIII.

The Story of My Beginnings

Whenever I turn a corner, as in a detective novel, and wake up in the little town of Samarkand, which, as you know, is on the disputed border between Massachusetts and Vermont, where traders often stop for the night, the stars forming a proper circle of blessing overhead, I remember a tale about squirrels that you used to tell me, as I was a child then and maybe even now.

It is only when you are standing in a mowed field on a farm in Southern Vermont, just over the border from Massachusetts, looking at the wreath of stars from the correct distance and angle, that you can delude yourself into thinking the shadows they cast don't move, and that the fire foretold in your ancestor's dream has stopped climbing the trees.

Samarkand is one town over from where the growing herd of mind readers is kept close together so as to jam their receptors, and just down the road from where poets are assigned a variety of menial tasks so as to not encourage them to happily succumb to untoward flights of fancy.

Samarkand has the only gate through which traders can pass—heading north—without surrendering portions of their hair for examination.

Samarkand is where insomniacs gather once a year and knit scarves for all the hours they were unable to dream—long black ribbons of wide-eyed frenzy.

Yesterday, I wanted to express my inner bloodstained charioteer but was able to resist the urge to paw deeper into the perfumed pleasures of my surroundings, as I lay on the ground looking up at the sky, waiting for the stars to fall, and the snow of their twinkling to cover me in stone.

Whenever I turn a corner, as on a street in Samarkand, and remember that I left my detective novel on the bus that brought me here, I begin retelling the tale of the fire and the trees it ate, angry and gluttonous in its crackling.

It is always best not to stand on a roof in the rain.

I want to grow up and be a street cleaner.

I want to grow up on cleaner streets.

I was born into a family that believed penguins and shadows lead a double life and that it was better to be surrounded by penguins than by shadows.

This is how I came to be a statue of a penguin in a black scarf greeting you at the northern gate of Samarkand.

This is how I came to be the shadow of a broken public fountain.

Genghis Chan on Drums

1.

Once you were a crescendo, a cascade, a sarabande
hacked haiku coughing up blood and spitting on moon
with no dance to cry over spilled sludge

Once your name was John Chinaman
You lived in a cricket ding-dong on outskirts of mills and malls
in granted state of Marshmallow Falls

You said, call me Johnny Jodhpurs or Lenny Systematic
Suave Stymie or Hamburger Harmonica

You said, listen to my thunderstorm and fire worm
while you perambulate squeal and stamp indissoluble

You said, I am a picket fence, a rumor, a superlative immigrant, a turboprop laxative

You said, pickax, influenza, rum, and tuxedo twang

This is the placard above my rickshaw chariot moon chaser swoop

2.

Once you were an egret tired of all regrets sticking to you like white feathers

You thought you were a mirage, a whisper, a lone lover standing on one leg,
a bush or shrub steamed in shimmering distance.

You began to dream that you saw what you were dreaming in front of you
as you looked down from airplane window

remembering the dog sitting beside your desk
two boys burning a rat for fun
a bank robbery in progress, and the song of a young girl
who lived beside her dead parents—another body
lives inside my dilapidated husk, another intruder
longing to leave me standing by the water's blue and pink edge
wondering why I can no longer see my face when I look down into the water

3.

Once you were a makeshift bamboo pontoon bride, a cleaver man
a phonograph of someone lost in an eddy that no one heard
a dirty look pushed through a window
a young girl standing on a stoop listening to her father spout clichés
as if they were precious nuggets to be handed down
from one military attaché to another

Winter came and stayed

You were scheduled to make a speech
until you saw a ghost had entered the auditorium and was sitting in the front row
smiling, your throat a furnace where the words bloomed in flames
a lamp of unstable considerations pressing its muddy towel against your bleeding gums

4.

Once you were human but then you forgot to put in for overtime
The weather grew hungry but you were not in the mood and decided
that being ignorant was a sign of how savvy you were at not being fooled

by those who talked down from the sky or wherever they sat
when they were not shitting on others besides you
there were many tragic cuckoos indebted to their illnesses
standing at the end of the street waiting to drift into the creviced sun's bright red scar

Once you were a greasy river cut off from dreams and hundreds of fish
floated on your back their bellies swollen and their heads stinking and you said
a hundred years from now this watch that I am looking at will still be telling time
even though it lies on the muddy bottom, a lone lantern pointing to the stars

Once you were a wall pockmarked with bullet holes
astonished that anyone would look at you and not vomit
but that was before the future arrived, an unexpected guest

Ed's and My Opinion

It was Ed Roberson
who told me

that white people were
the color of pork

which would have
upset my mother

because she believed
that pork was superior

to all other meats
but that white people

had not done anything
to improve the world

Irascible old Chinaman
becoming ever more

unacceptable in
appearance and speech

If you don't know English,
where else can you go

in this shrinking panorama
jerks shrieking falling sky

The three wise Chinaman
have been filled in

by a different crayon
than the pink pork sticks

known as "flesh-colored."
Have you ever gotten

to know a Chinaman
who did not shit

for his country
or raise a holy stink

I don't like the way
they eat during holidays

I think cats do something
similar in alleyways

We are not sure what
materials they are made of

Surely nonflammable
and safe to chew on

Untitled

Am I a wooden soldier
who lost his way
to the match factory

a fat man
who got stuck
inside an ice cream truck

a novelist who ran
into a valley
without any words

Is this why
I cannot
write you a poem

Untitled (Hotel)

The blue moon is not quivering, I am

Of heavenly flowers planted, fall, and stick

Sins or since, what does time matter

Now that I have so little left in which to dream

Tangled as I am, I do not want to leave

Inflamed quagmire illuminating my brief stay

So much of it spent dreaming of you

I have, in my own eyes, become laughable

To think my thinking matters a whit in this wind

Living in a hotel room only I have a key to

Not even the owners know that I am here

Dwelling on outskirts of town

I am not a stranger to my own thoughts

There is no footage to save, no photographs

Certainly not the clump of dust I am to become

After I Turn Sixty-Nine (Third Attempt)

I will never be a natty gumshoe sitting in Sandusky waiting for a bowl of peach cobbler
I will never be shot out of a cannon for the amusement of others
I will never join a woodpecker in an intermittent percussive search for protein
I will think differently about foul emissions and bodily eruptions from this day hence
I will not laugh at you for talking to an animal as if it is the last of its kind
I will never again copulate with the same vigor that once surprised and worried me
I will try and burn whatever may be construed as a statement of personal disappointment
I will not get up from my chair and begin to twist and shout or so I say now
I will watch children laughing at me for a variety of reasons, some of them cruel
I will no longer look into a camera and pretend to be serious example
I will not tell you that I am a frail exhalation walking under a cloud of capricious turmoil
I will no longer think that diapers are items from my distant past
I will try to use the words "loathsome" and "crypt" at least once a day
I will silently disagree with the poet who says a throw of the dice abolishes chance

For the Spirit of Jean Vigo

I began this poem shortly after I asphyxiated the cuckoo hiding in my alarm clock
I will never lift up a spoon of alphabet soup, even from languages I do not comprehend
I wish to be described as a nuisance who acts with sincerity and dedication
I refuse to turn a buttery shade of pale in order to improve my complexion
I like to thumb through books that have no spines and their covers are burned
I welcome the snow widening its cavalcade on the charcoal-colored horizon
I neither sweep my plumed hat before me nor grab the hilt of my sword
I will not open my mouth and reveal how many rows of teeth I possess
I always make my bed, even when I do not leave it and go to my boring job
I like poems that perspire freely, fart ferociously, and urinate dreamily
I cannot tolerate another winter in a fallout shelter wondering where the time went
I will give you all my personal stationery if you promise never to write me
I loot because you proudly put it on display and act like I am not supposed to take it
I do not wish to be exonerated by you or anyone else

(Written on June 4, 2020, the day before my 70th birthday)

After Crossing the Mountains in Montale

Vain old man soon in need of a plaid diaper and blue eyes
Where do you think you are headed now that you have come alive

Is that hag talking to me or I am hearing voices in my other head again
When will I be marked as spam, Internet space junk, added weight

Is this the only way you know how to turn life's constant nightmare
into a leaky faucet from which this poem flows, trickles, or drips

Depending on the carcass bubbling inside you
its turtledoves settling on memory's quivering artery

You have not exploited the only worthwhile song
I have ever sung into the mouth of a yawning cat

Which is another name for sunset in this valley of housing projects
where children grow up to be robot operators in essential industries

I tried meeting you on another plane but I was unable to call you there
Today, my poem is a spitball thrown at the eye of a hurricane

After Rilke

I would describe myself
as a flinty expression

found in remnant
pile of sacked sky

an unrepeatable
self-designed

tattoo
card

I want to upload
these images

to the Internet
the hereafter of heaven

never complete
already infinite

Porous
poor us

or pour
us

I want
to stay

in this
place

a little different
than before

Why I Am Still a Poet

I have never worn pantaloons and a tricorn hat to a poetry reading
I have never claimed to embrace multitudes or platitudes
I have never had my name on an A-list, even as an alternate
I have never shared photos of myself with my head shaved
I do not do handstands to prove I can still get it up
I do not teach Creative Writing in a prestigious program
I do not write about the woes that befall me and make my suffering special
I did not perform a weather report to prove my avant-garde credentials
I do not serve up saccharine dollops that would make a goldfish gag
I did not stand in a piazza and declare that I was a lunatic comet or failed comic
I did not compare my mother to the moon gnawed at by a pillar of salt
I did not press the accelerator while pointing at the stars and singing your name
I do not mind being ostracized if it means I am like everyone else
I sit in the dark and tell jokes to my dog until night fills my windows

Abecedarian with Stutter, Written on Bathroom Wall of the Apocalypse Lounge

Another alphabet soup brimming with poisoned hieroglyphs

Battle decay settles its wet fingers on your cold shoulder

COMING SOON: Lie detectors for palm readers

Delighted by ravings written in cubbyholes of Bedlam

Edited lines in moldy treatises, forged journals, and plagiarized biographies

Found gasping in field of overturned monuments and dead squirrels

Greater disappointments await you until further notice

How enchanting your shiny shackles can be at a time like this

I will match your abstinence and raise you one tiny guffaw

Join together and plead for a snowball's chance at being granted temporary status

Kafka dreamed he was chained to a tricycle tied to a burning tree

Luckily, mortification is the least of your afflictions

My protuberances have enthralled clowns of every stripe and polka dot

Noxious, Nebraska welcomes all nomads crawling across the unmarked plains

Over my dead loaf and don't you forget it, ever

Patron head-bashing is no longer consider necessary for admission

Queen Spending Spree and Mister Smarty Pants have started their descent

Refresh the parts of yourself that manage to remain intact

Start over—an alphabet soup full of brittle lice

Scurrilous Sleaze with a twist of bristling lemon

Saul and the Abyssinians singing in a tree, P-I-S-S-I-N-G

The young policeman begins barking relentlessly at approaching strangers

Under the weather, volcano, boardwalk, and skin

Verisimilitude and its shadow wink back at you

What lowly sow licked your face, Mr. Prune Apple

Xenomorphic wildlife in easily disposable jars, all yours for only a fraction of a lifetime

Yearning for a cheeseburger and fries when a can of worms will have to do

Zephyrs have started nudging this zeppelin toward the lightning storm

Call to Prayer

Let us jeer all the officials
the muckety-mucks and know-it-alls
the city councilors, chairmen,
and presidents of the board

Let us make funny faces
whenever we are asked
to pause and listen
to one of their public announcements

Let us laugh long and heartily
whenever they somberly say
that they are with us
that they are sending us

their heartfelt prayers
their deepest condolences
their wishes for a speedy recovery

Let us hoot, like drunken owls
Let us be loud and obstreperous
Let us cackle, again and again

IX.

Catullus Sails to China (1)

Now that my sojourn is circling a drain
Should I slow this engine down and wash
Moon's lacquered thermos and cold hair
What did I think I could possibly gain
When I sank into reams of grainy and gripe
What did I dream the stars would grant me
For wandering into every squall of petty grievance
All promises of sweet return posted in evening air
All melons and dates grown beside the Bosphorus
Sent here, wrapped in blue sky of Chinese paper
Catullus, you dented pumpkin, you must halt
This idiocy and calculate the loss you see as lost
A handful of little goodbyes might be necessary
Admit what everyone knows—you are an ungodly child

Catullus Sails to China (2)

When did you sink to amateur
In tide pools of love's red wake
Waiting for her to love you in the dark
Listen, my yawning droopy snake,
There are no talismans to enhance
The rhythms of a drunken night
No wide vulture to lift you from the dead
You have become what you once laughed at—
A wet rag crammed under a pile of puppets
Shall I make a smile to fit your tired mouth
Whoever loves you will fail to change this
As good at math as you like to brag
Can you calculate the exact loss
Your arms are about to embrace

Catullus Sails to China (3)

Will we ever be more than gifts to the dead
Buckets of ash tossed into sea's grinding claws
Last night, my friend invited the Toothless
Over for peacock platter and honeyed wine
What does Mister Old Glue do to inflame
The remains of his decrepit body like that
Get out of your clothes—we must commit
This misdemeanor as fast as possible
We are no tarrying brother and sister
Sorry, Old and Borrowed, but I have
To work with you on the best of days
Get out of your clothes—Let merciful gods
Bestow blessings on my little moniker
My poor dumb bird, now swollen and crying red

Catullus Sails to China (4)

Leisure is a boilermaker sitting opposite you
I no longer count those who drowned
In my riches, leaving their bones
To wash up on a terracotta floor
Listen, a broken bed can be given a new neck
No, no, no, this poem is for you
Before you dump me in the old people's park
Just another bad deposit on view
Or must you say more insulting things about me
Is it something other than my flailing eyes
That shuffles my interest into your hair
The sounds stay buried in your curled mouth
My luck, I never get to think of you as a beast
I love that we are not married and we are a nightmare

Catullus Sails to China (5)

Dear Anticipation, the gods deceive the people
Into thinking they are ready for longevity
Offering them pedestals and flattering hormones
This is why I stole myself away from the world
Why I pretended to be an indifferent miser
This is how to entrust things to mediocre minds
Let them be angry and ungrateful—Why torment yourself
Why clean your lips of the words you hold back
Fomenting against more stupid love, chest heaving
I love you so unhappy I could violate the treaty
We made when we pretended to be frolicking children
Is your husband starting to rise up again
Send him to the house of the eternally ugly
I love you so unhappy I am wearing myself out

Catullus Sails to China (6)

Listen to the voice in your head, Catullus
Not the one sitting next to you draining mojitos
Negronis, updated sidecars, bubbling volcanoes
Of yum-filled drops of deliciousness
That cannot be replicated, which is why
You have to have one, not that the nitwit
Ignoramus dunderhead roller coaster
Parked next to you knows mojo from juju
Which is why he was hexed from birth
No silver spoon, no baby shoe dipped in gold
Just a plastic bucket for a head,
You don't need to cut someone's throat
To know that he bleeds and the blood isn't worth
The factory-made carpet it drips on

Catullus Sails to China (7)

When will you admit you are a louse
Roped Catullus, who keeps squandering
Every chance of love that comes your way
You must want to fall out of the sky
Your ass illuminated by clouds and fire
You sing: Lend me another thousand kisses
My mouth is hungry and I am poor
Yes, let's send a postcard to our love
Stuck on a raft, crammed with cursed blessings
I will no longer carry you back to the table
Instead, I will shout—Skunk, return, return
To unclean monotony and masturbation
Come back, when you are comfortable and spruced up
When the moon is not a bloody mouth asking to be kissed

Catullus Sails to China (8)

Now that you have attained baboon status
Catullus, and become a failed circus act
Did you ever think about the reverberations
Emanating from your bodily transmissions
In the cycle of take this and take that
Maybe it is time to start looking for a lighthouse
Where you can scale your ladders of harbored anger
No tooth and half tooth are old scars
Whenever your passion begins lighting its flare
Another row of buttons floats outside your path
Wandering between a warm bed and bad thoughts
Banjos, red underwear, and headlong satisfaction
Dearest Sparrow, I once again prove myself
To be another faraway friend that no longer exists

Catullus Sails to China (9)

Not my most indelicate verses—this grumbling
I keep that pride of curses in a well-fed yard
But I will tell you this: my eyes are starting to see
Every blemish of forget-me-knots and cobwebs
Tugging me toward my stooped pile
With broken bones and face my green lot
Bold sum: wouldn't you rather date a bodiless bot
And not waste sweat with this card-carrying member
Stuck out, breathing sweet tongue shoe in place
I say, I am not half the fan of fire I should be
I say, how else can I exit hell's infinite coliseum
Icy bosons piercing night's spreading flush
My mouth of vile gabbing at legions of ghosts
While I keep swimming in hot delirium

Catullus Sails to China (10)

I will go to my farm and open
A huge bath in my chest
And wash away the last
Disorders of my rubbled heart
When you grow old
You inevitably become foolish
Begin making oaths to everyone's air
Just another donkey declaiming at lunch
A man with no teeth and less hair
A wrinkled example of what you used to be
Instant food gone bad in a bag
Inside some men sits a cake and an egg, but not you
I used to tell elaborate jokes, and now I am one
The green cities of Asia await me

Epilogue

Nursery Song
(After Sean Bonney)

Don't say "pandemic lockdown"
Say Fuck the rich/their private island getaways
Say Fuck their Aspen lodges/stocked with climate-controlled volcanoes
and children named after weather stations and rare cheeses

Don't say "clubbed and beaten"
Say Fuck clubbing and slumming
Say Fuck following and liking

Don't say "assortment of pretty much everything you can imagine,
at a loss for words, beyond your wildest dreams"
Don't say "quartz countertops, home theater, private cul-de-sac, second getaway"
Say Fuck the rich, their carbon footprint, their dinosaur ways

Don't say "stay at home orders, essential workers, front lines of death,"
Say Fuck fabulous gym rat, TV personality smile, life style influencer

Don't say "drowning in debt, jobless rollout, prioritize assisted living,"
Say Fuck lounging by the pool, swimming into the future, moonlight stroll

Don't say "another milestone, strain capacity, possible spread,"
Say Fuck galas and red carpets
Fuck blockbusters and special consultants
Fuck jewel in social crown
Fuck emulation and following in footsteps
Fuck controversial outfits glowing in the dark
Fuck svelte gluttony and perfect abs

Don't say "going hungry"
Say Fuck jaw dropping

Don't say "hoi polloi, riffraff, and proles"
Don't say "back to normal or the way things used to be"
Don't say "Let's see what the future holds"
Say Fuck the little golf cart/stretch limo they rode in on
Say Fuck their followers and their driveling ways
Don't say "viral", say virus
Say Fuck your pumpkin spice

Don't say "comfortable at-home attire, loungewear, soon to be biggest trends"
Say Fuck whole new meaning and affordable chic

Don't say "The right balm for wardrobe doldrums"
Don't say "fashion plate and ice cream-colored costume"
Don't say "luxury matching designer errands"
Say Fuck the old self, the complete overhaul, destroy all evidence of inner calm

Don't say "stable environment, outdoor grounds, privacy, and for the kids"
Don't say, "pitchfork diplomacy, flag stabbing, constitutional gripes"
Say Fucking bloody thorn in your side, I got nowhere to go but up

Nursery Song (Second Chorus)

Fuck "flaunt"

Fuck "perfectly my type" and "got to go for what you want"

Fuck "meant to be" and "forever"

Fuck "haven't stopped smiling"

Fuck "has my back" and "always there for me"

Fuck "effortlessly demure" and "naturally handsome"

Fuck "sincere apologies"   "no excuses"   and "the single worst decision of my life"

Fuck "celebrity breeding" and "predicting children's looks"

Fuck "epic blunder"

Fuck "steamy"   "dreamy"   and "creamy"

Fuck "debut selfie tribute"

Fuck "plant-based workout"

Fuck, "heartfelt"   "double take"   and "in a frenzy"

Fuck "fist bumps" and "baby bumps"

Fuck "one rule for celebrities and one for everyone else"

Fuck "binge"   "fringe"   and "cringe"

Fuck "wonderful journey" and "eager to begin the next chapter"

Notes

(P. 55) The phrase "Bloken Exhaust" was lifted from *Wobble Factory* by Anselm Berrigan. The poem is dedicated to him.

(P. 92) "Poem" is for Clark Coolidge.

(P. 95) "After Edmund Spenser" derives all its end words, minus the subtraction of one letter, from "Sonnet 75," which begins, "One day I wrote her name upon the strand."

(P. 96) "Suite from an English-Arabic Dictionary" is for Ahmani Fahmy.

Acknowledgments

I want to thank the following magazines and editors for giving my poems a place to exist both physically and digitally:

Big Other, Café Review, Chicago Review, Colorado Review, Conjunctions, Hambone, Harper's, Journal of New Jersey Poets, Manoa, Massachusetts Review, Mrkgnao, Mudfish, 1111, On the Seawall, Paris Review, Poem-a-Day, Salt, The Brooklyn Rail, Verse Daily, Vestiges, Volt.

Alessandro Porco, Nathaniel Mackey, John Madera, Monica Youn, Mathew Cooperman, Joseph Lease, Ben Lerner, Gilian Conoley, Jill Hoffman, Bradford Morrow, Ron Slate, Anselm Berrigan, James Capozzi, Ellen Doré Watson, J. P. Dancing Bear, Jared Daniel Fagen, Frank Stewart, Billie Chernicoff, Steve Luttrell.

"Genghis Chan on Drums" appeared in the Foundation of Contemporary Arts 2020 Annual Grants booklet. Thanks to Stacy Tenenbaum Stark and the FCA.

I am very grateful to the following editors for selecting my work:

Paisley Rekdal, editor of *Best American Poetry 2020* (New York: Scribner, 2020)

Tracy K. Smith, editor of *Best American Poetry 2021* (New York: Scribner, 2021)

Paul Munden, Alvin Pang, and Shane Strange, editors of *No News: 90 Poets Reflect in a Unique BBC Broadcast* (ACT: Australia, Recent Work Press, 2020)

Many thanks and much more go to the following intrepid and generous individuals:

Kreg Hasegawa for designing and publishing *Annals of a Gumshoe* (with drawings by Trevor Winkfield) (Smoke Specs, 2019)

Sydney Jean Reisen for designing, handsetting, and printing *Catullus Sails to China* (Olchef Press, 2020)

Essye Klempner for designing, printing, and publishing *Bloken Exhaust* (with drawings by Branden Koch) (Ink Cap Press, 2020)

Tammy Nguyen for designing and printing a letterpress broadside of "Why I Am Still a Poet" for the Center of Book Arts 2021 Virtual Benefit honoring Alison Knowles

About the Author

John Yau is the author of many books of poetry, fiction, and criticism. His most recent book of poetry is *Bijoux in the Dark* (2018). Alongside these publications, he has written many monographs and contributed to numerous catalogs and museum publications. In 2012, he cofounded the online publication *Hyperallergic Weekend*. He received a Rabkin Prize for his art critictsm in 2021, the 2018 Jackson Poetry Prize, which is given annually to an American poet by Poets and Writers, and been recognized by the John Simon Guggenheim Memorial Foundation, National Endowment of the Arts, Academy of American Poets, New York Foundation of the Arts, and the Foundation for Contemporary Arts for his poetry and fiction. His poems and criticism have been translated into French, Chinese, Spanish, German, Italian, Romanian, Polish, Portuguese, and Korean. His work has been published in many magazines, including *Harper's Magazine*, *Poetry*, *BOMB*, *Partisan Review*, *Paris Review*, *Hambone*, *Denver Quarterly*, and the *Colorado Review*. His poems have been selected to appear in the yearly anthology, *Best American Poetry* in 1988, 2000, 2002, 2020, and 2021. In 1999, he started the small press, Black Square Editions, which has published more than fifty books of poetry, fiction, essays, and translations from French, Chinese, Spanish, and German. His collaborations with artists, such as Thomas Nozkowski, Pat Steir, Archie Rand, Chuck Webster, Kathy Barry, Jürgen Partenheimer, Kazuki Nakahara, and Richard Tuttle, are in the collection of numerous institutions, including the Museum of Modern Art, New York; Whitney Museum of American Art; New York Public Library; and the National Library of the Netherlands, He has been named a Chevalier in the Order of Arts and Letters by the French government, and has received the Distinguished Alumni Award from Brooklyn College (Class of 1978) and an honorary doctorate from the College of Creative Studies in Detroit. He has taught at the University of California, Berkeley, Munich Fine Art Academy, and is currently a Professor of Critical Studies at Mason Gross School of the Arts (Rutgers University). He lives in New York.

Genghia Chan on Drums
John Yau

Cover art: Charles Yuen, "Well of Tears," 78 x 69 inches,
oil on canvask, 2003, collection of Clifford Diver,
Lewes, Delaware. By permission of the artist.

Cover & interior design: Shanna Compton

Printed in the United States
by Books International, Dulles, Virginia
On Glatfelter 50# Cream Natures Book 440 ppi
Acid Free Archival Quality Recycled Paper

Publication of this book was made possible in part by gifts from
Katherine & John Gravendyk in honor of Hillary Gravendyk,
Francesca Bell, Mary Mackey, and The New Place Fund

Omnidawn Publishing
Oakland, California
Staff and Volunteers, Spring 2021

Rusty Morrison & Ken Keegan, senior editors & co-publishers
Kayla Ellenbecker, production editor & poetry editor
Gillian Olivia Blythe Hamel, senior editor & book designer
Trisha Peck, senior editor & book designer
Rob Hendricks, Omniverse editor, marketing editor, fiction editor & post-pub editor
Sharon Zetter, poetry editor & book designer
Liza Flum, poetry editor
Matthew Bowie, poetry editor
Anthony Cody, poetry editor
Jason Bayani, poetry editor
Juliana Paslay, fiction editor
Gail Aronson, fiction editor
Laura Joakimson, marketing assistant for Instagram & Facebook, fiction editor
Ashley Pattison-Scott, executive assistant & Omniverse writer, fiction editor
Ariana Nevarez, marketing assistant & Omniveres writerm, fiction editor